3/13

ENDER'S WORLD

D0068617

FRESH PERSPECTIVES ON THE SF CLASSIC

ENDER'S GAME

EDITED BY

Orson Scott Card

THREE RIVERS PUBLIC LIBRARY
25207 W. CHANNON DRIVE
P.O. BOX 300
CHANNAHON, IL 60410-0300

An Imprint of BenBella Books, Inc.
Dallas, Texas

"How It Should Have Ended" © 2013 by Eric James Stone
"The Monster's Heart" © 2013 by John Brown
"The Cost of Breaking the Rules" © 2013 by Mary Robinette Kowal
"Winning and Losing in *Ender's Game*" © 2013 by Hilari Bell
"Parallax Regained" © 2013 by David Lubar and Alison S. Myers
"Mirror, Mirror" © 2013 by Alethea Kontis
"Size Matters" © 2013 by Janis Ian
"Rethinking the Child Hero" © 2013 by Aaron Johnston
"A Teenless World" © 2013 by Mette Ivie Harrison
"Ender on Leadership" © 2013 by Tom Ruby
"Ender Wiggin, USMC" © 2013 by John F. Schmitt
"The Price of Our Inheritance" © 2013 by Neal Shusterman
"If the Formics Love Their Children Too" © 2013 by Ken Scholes
"*Ender's Game*: A Guide to Life" © 2013 by Matt Nix
"Introduction" and Q&As © 2013 by Orson Scott Card

All rights reserved. No part of this book may be used or reproduced in any
manner whatsoever without written permission except in the case of brief
quotations embodied in critical articles or reviews.

BenBella Books, Inc.
10300 N. Central Expressway, Suite 530 | Dallas, TX 75231
www.benbellabooks.com | Send feedback to feedback@benbellabooks.com

Printed in the United States of America
10 9 8 7 6 5 4 3 2 1

Library of Congress Cataloging-in-Publication Data is available for this title.
978-1-937856-21-2

Copyediting by Debra Kirkby, Kirkby Editorial Services
Proofreading by Michael Fedison and James Fraleigh
Cover illustration © 2012 by Nick Greenwood
Cover design by Jarrod Taylor
Text design and composition by Yara Abuata, Silver Feather Design
Printed by Berryville Graphics, Inc.

Distributed by Perseus Distribution | www.perseusdistribution.com
To place orders through Perseus Distribution:
Tel: 800-343-4499 | Fax: 800-351-5073
E-mail: orderentry@perseusbooks.com

Significant discounts for bulk sales are available. Please contact Glenn
Yeffeth at glenn@benbellabooks.com or 214-750-3628.

3 1561 00287 3515

CONTENTS

INTRODUCTION

ORSON SCOTT CARD

I thought I had a pretty good story when I gave my first draft of the original novelet "Ender's Game" to my mother to type up for submission.

My mother had been another set of eyes on all my plays and my handful of previous stories. So even though I had long been a very fast and accurate typist myself, I passed her my longhand manuscript because I wanted to see how the story would work for her. This was my first serious attempt to write a sci-fi story to sell. My theatre company was getting good attendance, but losing money even with no rent and no salaries to pay (you can lose money on hit plays). I needed "Ender's Game" to help me launch a non-theatrical writing career. As a non-fan of sci-fi, my mother would definitely let me know if I had something that would work outside the science fiction community.

I was surprised at how strongly positive her reaction was. She had enjoyed my Worthing stories, but those were completely character-centered, with not a single space-ship and, for that matter, no electricity or power tools or weapons beyond a medieval level. They felt like fantasy. So "Ender's Game" was the first time I had asked my mother to read something that really felt like science fiction.

It wasn't the space stuff that worked for her. It was the child under pressure, isolated and yet able to build a community around him, able to keep his head and think inventively even when problems seemed impossible to everyone else. It was the human story.

It still is. Even as I adapted the story to novel length ten years later, and then spent another decade trying to distill the story into a form that would work for film, I never got confused about the source of the story's power.

Ender's Game does not work because it's sci-fi, or even a war story. Nor does it work in spite of those things. *Ender's Game* works because it is a story of the individual within the community.

The great dilemma of human life is that we are all strangers in a strange land. Genetically we are disposed to be communitarian. Even the worst misanthrope needs human company, hungers for it.

And no matter how individualistic we are, no matter how self-motivated, other people have strange and terrible powers over us. They can fill us with joy just by saying completely stupid things like "Good job" or "You were so cool." We are so hungry for the approval of the community that a pat on the back from someone we despise still makes us feel good. Even if we're ashamed of feeling good, we feel it.

It's like our innate response to little children. We feel protective. That's why the most terrible sound when a plane is landing is *not* the creaking of fatigued metal—it's the sound of a baby crying at the ear pain that results from the changing air pressure of landing. And when, in a play or movie, they show a child crying abjectly, our hearts stir with sympathy even when we know that untalented, cynical writers are manipulating us—because the survival of the human race depends on our passing along the gene that makes empathy for children a deep, abiding attribute of humans.

Yeah, that's part of the appeal of *Ender's Game*, too, and don't you forget it. *Ender's Game* works most powerfully when we see Ender *as a child*.

But more important than Ender Wiggin's status as a child is the fact that, regardless of age, he is an individual who is systematically *excluded* from the very community that he is required to save.

When Graff and Rackham, each in his own way, work to isolate Ender Wiggin, they know what they're doing. *Nothing* could possibly stress this child more than breaking off his connection with other people. So why do they do it? How will this help him?

Battle School is not about training soldiers, it's about training *war leaders*, people who can guide the soldiers— the bravest and strongest of a community's members—to risk their lives and commit terrible acts of killing in order to promote the survival and growth of the community.

In the testing that determines who is fit for command, it is vital that the selected candidates have a powerful sense of the importance of the community. That translates into a deep hunger to belong, an ability to love and care for others, strong empathy, and a willingness to sacrifice for the genuine good of others.

But it is just as vital that they be able to *send other soldiers off to die*.

Weigh that in the balance for a moment. If you have war leaders who cannot bear to risk their soldiers' lives, *you will lose* to a determined enemy.

But if you have war leaders who do not treasure and value the lives of their soldiers, you will waste them. If I were writing one of the essays in this book, I would now overwhelm you with examples of both kinds of flawed leaders from world history. Instead, I will simply say that because Ender Wiggin was so extreme in his ability to love others and identify with them, it was highly likely that he would be unable to put them at risk.

Part of what protected Ender from this weakness was keeping from him the knowledge that the "games" he played had real consequences—that soldiers were dying as a result of his decisions.

But they could not be sure that he would not guess. Besides, part of what makes a great commander is imagination; even if he does not know the blips on the simulator screen are real ships with real pilots inside, he knows that they *represent* real pilots. Cold calculation tells him not to waste resources like ships uselessly; vivid imagination tells him these blips are pretending to be pilots, and he can't let any of them die.

So whether he guesses or imagines the reality of the pilots, Graff and Rackham want to instill in him the hard scars of social injury. Resentment, if you will: The sense that no matter how much you do for other people, they don't really love you or understand you; you are, ultimately, on your own. Those are the scars (they think) that will allow Ender to overcome his natural empathy.

But for me, there is another effect of Ender's isolation that his teachers did not really anticipate, but which affected him far more powerfully: the matter of delay. Without the teachers' actions that isolated him, Ender would very quickly have joined in as a valued member of the wider community of Battle School. He would have *fit right in*.

This would have left his most important leadership skill—the ability to *form* communities—undeveloped, atrophied. It is only because he is deliberately excluded from the normal wider community that he is forced to make a community out of misfits like Shen, and then gradually win over hostile or rejecting competitors like Alai and then Bernard.

Bonzo, who is no fool, sees at once what Ender Wiggin is: his ultimate rival. Not in the standings of the Battle Room games—though Bonzo *thinks* that's what he cares about. Bonzo knows, unconsciously, that he is not a good leader. That's why he is so desperate to build esprit de corps inside his own army. He does not know how it's done, but he can sense in Ender Wiggin a rival who *does* know how to do it.

Indeed, I think Bonzo hates Ender at once precisely because *he himself is drawn to Ender*. Bonzo, who fears and resents all rivals, finds Ender to be someone that he wants to follow. Bonzo senses, from the first moment, and at a level far deeper than his conscious mind can penetrate, that if he accepts Ender for a moment, Ender will quickly become the real leader of Bonzo's army.

Some people sense Ender's innate power to build communities and lead them, yet resist his attraction without trying to destroy him—I think of Dink Meeker, for instance, and Bean himself. But Bonzo is so driven by fear of failure—no, by fear of *shame*—that his only possible response to this powerful rival for the love of his own army is to destroy him, marginalize him, eliminate him.

Even when he gets Ender out of his army, it's under circumstances that expose Bonzo to shame and ridicule. Bonzo feels himself to be excluded from the praise and acceptance of the wider community, and this injury strikes deep—for there is no worse injury human beings can sustain. Gossip really is the cruelest weapon; people frequently *die* rather than expose themselves to shame in front of the community to which they have the greatest allegiance.

When Bonzo was isolated, he responded with hatred and rage; it brought out the worst in him, made him a bully, forced him to build his community out of the worst soldiers he could find.

When Ender was isolated, he accepted his nonacceptance to a point, but then found the best people who were *not* rejecting him and made a community—and then an army—out of *them*.

Giving Ender an army made of talented misfits, as the teachers (and, as we learn from *Ender's Shadow*, Bean) did, was the ideal answer to Ender's pain: He thrived best when he was working to bring out the best in other people.

This was his fundamental technique of community formation. People followed him not because he flattered them or made them feel temporary enthusiasms or bribed them or bragged to them. They followed him because they could see that he *cared* about them and that, by submitting to his discipline, *they got better*.

This is what flattering or bribing would-be leaders misunderstand. These techniques work up to a point, but in the end, the people following you because you supply these things to them will be *ashamed* of following you.

But when you follow a leader who demands the best from you, and helps you become better than you were, you are *proud* to become a part of the community led by him.

Even ambitious fellow-students in Battle School realized that their best chance of excelling, not just inside the school but later, beyond it, was to follow Ender Wiggin, to do what he taught them, and to imitate him as best they could.

So what Ender created, because the teachers isolated him from the larger community, was a community of the kind of people who aspire to be better than they are. Not to *seem* better, but to *be* better. His isolation allowed him to find the cream of the cream.

Yet throughout the story, he has to face the cruel truth about human life. Those who joined his community, sustained by his love and feeling themselves grow greater because they were with him, received something that Ender could not possibly receive himself. The community he formed was real, and felt real to all who belonged to it. But where Ender could assure *them* that they belonged, that they were worthy, who was there to assure Ender himself?

It is possible to be a powerful leader of a community you formed yourself, to be seen by all who are in that community as the best of them, the inmost point of their sphere—and yet to feel yourself to be outside it. Ender did not feel himself to be inside this community and sustained by it. He felt himself to be like Atlas, straining to hold up this orb, this sphere, this world, but never capable of being *of* or *in* that world.

Even when the teachers stopped isolating him, it remained true. Even if Ender had been allowed to return to Earth, it would have been true. He would never, never have felt himself to belong... because there was no one greater or stronger than himself who could admit him, sustain him—to whom he could wholly give himself.

That's why it was so vital that, in writing *Speaker for the Dead*, I make the family of Marcão Ribeira *real*, not just to the readers, but to Ender himself. Here was a community that he did not form himself. A family that was *not* his. And instead of dividing it and remaking it with himself at the center, he carefully and delicately *joined* it. When the children accepted him in the place of their father, it gave him something he could never have otherwise had: a community, larger than himself, which accepted him as a full member, yet which he had not created and did not hold up like Atlas.

That is why *Ender's Game* is such a delicate thing, which I have never been able to make again in my other books, though early in my career I certainly tried. Before I understood why it worked, I tried imitating all the superficial aspects of *Ender's Game* (for instance, in "Mikal's Songbird" and "Unaccompanied Sonata"); the results were stories as good as any I know how to write, which nevertheless failed to find the same kind of resonance that *Ender's Game* has achieved with many, but by no means all, of those who have read it.

Ender's Game did not sweep the world all at once. It reached a certain number of people very powerfully. The short story was the only reason I received the John W. Campbell Award for best new science fiction writer the year after it was published; the novel went on to win the Hugo and Nebula, because it was so intensely successful with those who liked it at all. But it was not a *majority* choice, merely a *plurality* choice (as such awards always are).

It still took more than two decades before *Ender's Game* ever appeared on a bestseller list, and then only because teachers, seeing the power it had for at least some of their students, required it for summer or school-year reading. There are many things worth discussing about the subject matter of the book—strategy and tactics in war, social rules, "love your enemy," literary form, childhood, parenting, educational theory, and more—but what makes it useful is primarily this: Even people who would never willingly pick up a sci-fi novel or a war novel understand that something in *Ender's Game* deals with the most important aspect of human life.

Few of us even know what that is; few of us understand how it shapes our own lives. But most of those to whom *Ender's Game* feels most important are those who, like me, feel themselves to be perpetually outside their most beloved communities, never able to come inside and feel confident of belonging. Loneliness is at the heart of *Ender's Game*, and the reason it works so well is because it carries with it the firm assurance that even though Ender *never* feels himself to belong, the reader knows he *does* belong, that he is the ultimate insider even though he stands outside.

Ender's Game is the story of the lonely hero who nevertheless *has value*, and because he never gets to enjoy that validation within the pages of the book, the reader feels a perpetual connection to Ender, a hunger to reach inside the pages and let this child receive that knowledge in his heart: You are one of us, you are the best of us, you speak for us.

No, subtract the "us." The readers who love *Ender's Game* most are those who do not believe they are part of any *us*, not really; they feel themselves to be like Ender in their isolation. They say to him: You are part of *me*, the best of *me*, you speak to *me*.

Did I know this when I wrote the book? Of course not. Not an inkling. I made my story choices because they felt important and true to me—that is the only method of making story choices that is worth anything to a writer. There are no formulas or archetypes that you can simply grab and plug into your story (or, worse, force your story to fit in with); it has to arise out of your own deepest inchoate hungers and understanding.

That was where *Ender's Game* came from, and to those who receive young Ender into their hearts whole-heartedly, I must say this: I am one of you.

HOW IT SHOULD HAVE ENDED

ERIC JAMES STONE

I grew up reading science fiction. My dad had a large collection of books written by authors from the Golden Age, so I read short stories and novels by Isaac Asimov, Robert A. Heinlein, A. E. van Vogt, and more. Stories about space flight and interstellar wars held a particular fascination for me—a fascination that continues to this day, as I love reading the Honor Harrington series by David Weber and the adventures of Lois McMaster Bujold's Miles Vorkosigan, among others.

One of the authors I enjoyed the most when I was young was Eric Frank Russell: the first science fiction novel I read was *The Space Willies*, and *Wasp* has remained one of my favorites to this day. Both those novels (and many other stories I read) involved clever humans outwitting aliens. The aliens might be more technologically advanced, they might have special powers, they might be more numerous, but in the end, we humans always figured out a way to defeat them. John W. Campbell's novella "Who Goes There?"—the basis of the movie *The Thing*—is a perfect example of that sort of story.

And that was the sort of story I thought I was getting when I started reading *Ender's Game*.

Actually, what I started reading was *Il gioco di Ender*. I first spotted the book in a train-station bookstore in Naples, and I picked it up to practice my Italian. Later, on reading the novel in English, I found that minor details came across differently in translation. For example, the formics were referred to as *i Scorpioni*, so I imagined them more like giant scorpions than giant ants. And because the word *porta* means both *gate* and *door*, my mind translated the key phrase "*La porta nemica è giù*" as "The enemy door is down." The correct English phrase still feels slightly wrong to me.

But the essentials of the story are the same in any language, and I loved *Ender's Game* from the first page. Here was not just a human but a child, who would ultimately need to outwit a technologically superior, telepathic race with an empire spanning dozens of worlds. Before he could get to that point, however, he had to win victory after victory, first in the Battle Room, and then in the simulator. I thrilled to read how he executed each of his cunning strategies. Seeing how he could adjust to whatever was thrown at him was a delight, and I loved the book all the way to Ender's victory at the formics' home world and the dramatic revelation that what had seemed to be simulations were actual battles.

If *Ender's Game* had ended there, it would have been one of my favorite books of all time, but something strange happened: the book didn't end. It kept going.

First, there is a war on Earth (and on Eros) that Ender essentially sleeps through because he is so depressed about winning the most important war in the history of the world. Then he does not even get to go home to Earth with all his friends from Battle School. Instead, he goes off to a colony world, where he finds the message the formics left for him, plus the pupal hive queen capable of re-establishing the species that had almost wiped out humanity. And not only does Ender not immediately smash the pupa to end the threat once and for all, he looks for a good place to let it give birth.

I finished the book in complete puzzlement. Why did Orson Scott Card ruin a perfectly good humans versus aliens book with all that weird stuff at the end?

—

A website called HowItShouldHaveEnded.com (HISHE for short) features animated short films that give alternate (and generally very funny) endings for movies. Of course, HISHE did not exist back when I first read *Ender's Game*—websites did not even exist yet. But if the equivalent of HISHE had existed for books, I would have been ready to explain how *Ender's Game* should have ended: with Ender's victory over the formics and the big reveal that he had actually been fighting the war. Sure, there could be a little denouement, maybe a triumphant medal ceremony like the one at the end of the original *Star Wars*, but I felt the story was essentially over with Ender's victory.

In fact, the original "Ender's Game" short story only had a couple of brief scenes after that victory when it was published in *Analog* magazine. When Card expanded the story into a novel to serve as the background story for *Speaker for the Dead*, he added a lot of material to the beginning of the story: the original began when Ender was already the leader of Dragon Army, so all the scenes involving Peter and Valentine, plus his first years at Battle School, were new for the novel. But Card also added several scenes at the end, including the war on Earth and Eros, and everything involving the colony world. The excuse that Card was using those final scenes to set things up for a sequel was not good enough. Did there need to be a bunch of extra scenes after blowing up the Death Star to set up *The Empire Strikes Back*? I felt what was in the novel should be able stand on its own terms, even if *Speaker for the Dead* had never been written.

There may not have been HISHE to do a spoof ending for *Ender's Game*, but there was someone who expressed my thoughts perfectly: "Take it up to the day [Ender] won the final battle. Stop it there. Nothing that [Ender did] since then is worth writing down."

That brilliant bit of analysis came from none other than Ender Wiggin himself, as he is talking to Valentine about her plan to write the story of his life.

So, case closed? The novel should have ended after Ender won?

In the words of Valentine, responding to Ender when he says nothing after winning the battle was worth writing down: "Maybe ... And maybe not."

—

The second time I read *Ender's Game*, I had a plan: I would only read the book up to where I thought it should have ended. That way, I would still get all the thrills of Ender's victories in the Battle Room and the war against the formics but would not have to bother with all that unnecessary stuff at the end. Call it *Ender's Game: The Good Parts Version*.

But when I reached that point in the novel, something strange happened: I wanted to keep reading.

What changed?

The first time I read the novel, I focused on the high-level story arc about the war between humans and formics. That was the story that fit my preconceptions of what the novel was about because it was the kind of story I had read before and loved: clever humans versus dangerous aliens. During that first read, I did not build up any sympathy for the formics; they were merely a threat that had to be eliminated. And although I loved Ender as a character, the aspect of his personality that seemed most important was his tremendous competence at outwitting his opponents. That high-level story arc came to its conclusion with the end of the formic wars.

However, when I was reading the novel for the second time, my preconceptions about the novel had already been broken. Knowing that the formics had realized their mistake and were not planning to attack humanity again allowed me to develop some sympathy for them during the course of the novel. I also began to see the importance of things that had merely been part of the background before, and I realized that there was a much more personal story arc involving Ender's character. That arc did not end with the climactic destruction of the formic home world. In fact, the high point of the war story arc coincides with the low point of the personal story arc, which is why Ender reacts to ultimate victory with deep depression.

—

The key to Ender's personal story arc can be found in the first chapter. He has just beaten Stilson—and Stilson's gang—by breaking the unwritten rules of fighting and savagely kicking the bully while he was down. His rationale for doing so is perfectly understandable, so we as readers do not see Ender himself as a bully. But the chapter ends with the following lines: "Ender leaned his head against the wall of the corridor and cried until the bus came. I am just like Peter. Take my monitor away, and I am just like Peter."

This introduces the central conflict of Ender's character: the fear that he is like Peter, his tormenter. The sentiment is repeated several times throughout the novel.

- After he accidentally breaks Bernard's arm on the shuttle up to the Battle School:

  I am Peter. I'm just like him. And Ender hated himself…I am not a killer, Ender said to himself over and over. I am not Peter. No matter what Graff says, I'm not. I was defending myself. I bore it a long time. I was patient. I'm not what he said.

- After he kills the Giant in the mind game: "I'm a murderer, even when I play. Peter would be proud of me."

- After he kills the snake in the tower in the mind game and then sees Peter's face when looking in a mirror:

  > This game knows too much about me. This game tells filthy lies. I am not Peter. I don't have murder in my heart. And then a worse fear, that he was a killer, only better at it than Peter ever was; that it was this very trait that pleased the teachers. It's killers they need for the bugger wars. It's people who can grind the enemy's face into the dust and spatter their blood all over space.

- When Valentine is talking to Graff about why Peter's face would have shown up in the game: "I told [Ender] that lots of times, you're not like Peter, you never like to hurt people, you're kind and good and not like Peter at all!"

- After Ender reads Valentine's letter:

  > Only then did he realize what he hated most about Val's letter. All that it said was about Peter. About how he was not at all like Peter. The words she had said so often as she held him, comforted him as he trembled in fear and rage and loathing after Peter had tortured him, that was all that the letter had said.

- As Ender is talking to Mazer after the victory over the formics: "I didn't want to kill them all. I didn't want to kill anybody! I'm not a killer! You didn't want me, you bastards, you wanted Peter, but you made me do it, you tricked me into it!"

That final one marks the emotional low point for Ender in the novel. Yes, he has won the greatest victory in the history of humanity, but he sees himself as having become what he feared the most: a cruel killer like Peter. Never mind that his mental view of Peter is an exaggerated version of the actual Peter; what matters is that he believes he has become like Peter, and that was the worst thing he could imagine becoming.

—

One of the best pieces of advice I have received about writing characters is that you should figure out what a character desires most—and what the character fears most. With that knowledge, you can craft a climax to the story that puts the desire and the fear into conflict. By making the stakes as high as possible on a personal level, the climax of the story is more powerful.

In Ender's case, the thing he desires most is to keep Valentine (and, by extension, the rest of humanity) safe by defeating the formics. It is that desire that motivates him to go to Battle School in the first place. Later, when he wanted just to quit and stay on Earth at the house by the lake, Graff brought in Valentine to remind Ender of what he was fighting for:

So that's why you brought me here, thought Ender. With all your hurry, that's why you took three months, to make me love Earth. Well, it worked. All your tricks worked. Valentine, too; she was another one of your tricks, to make me remember that I'm not going to school for myself. Well, I remember.

And of course, Ender's greatest fear is that he will become like Peter.

The climax of the novel juxtaposes that desire and that fear—even though, in a fascinating departure from the formula, Ender himself does not know that this is what is happening. He has no idea that his final battle is not a simulation, so it is not until after it is over that, for him, the desire and fear are both realized: he has saved Valentine from the formics but at the cost of (from his point of view) becoming a killer like Peter.

The climax of *Ender's Game* is so powerful not just because of the large-scale stakes of the war arc— the survival of humanity itself and the extinction of an alien race. It is powerful because at the same moment, there is a crucial turning point for Ender's personal stakes—the desire to save Valentine and the fear of becoming like Peter. What could have been simply another military triumph by the forces of humanity over the aliens, a story told many times before and since, becomes much more complex when juxtaposed with Ender's internal conflict.

So it is no wonder that Ender finds himself overwhelmed when he finds out the truth.

—

Fortunately, after his initial horror at what he has done wears off, Ender begins to pull out of his depression. After Alai surprises him in his quarters and he gets up ready to fight, he realizes he's probably going to be okay because "I thought you were about to kill me, and I decided to kill you first. I guess I'm just a killer to the core. But I'd rather be alive than dead."

The last sentence is actually about more than simply his own personal reaction to what he thought might be someone coming to attack him in his room. It's a declaration of his sanity regarding what he was tricked into doing: when it comes right down to it, Ender (and humans in general) would rather be alive than dead, and he understands that the survival of the human species is more important than his qualms about being a killer like Peter.

But Ender merely accepting the necessity of what he did is not a satisfactory conclusion to his personal character arc. He may have been tricked into killing all the formics, but he bears guilt for the results of his actions, and he needs a way to redeem himself: to atone for what he did and prove to himself that he is not Peter.

When Valentine invites him to go with her to help colonize a former formic world, Ender thinks he has found some small way to atone: "I'm going because I know the buggers better than any other living soul, and maybe if I go there I can understand them better. I stole their future from them; I can only begin to repay by seeing what I can learn from their past."

Of course, he then gets the opportunity to do far more than that to redeem himself By telling the formics' story through his Speaker for the Dead persona, Ender has the chance to redeem the entire formic race in the eyes of humans. (In the sequels, we find out that has the effect of changing the public perception of Ender from savior to monster, but that is irrelevant to his arc in this novel.)

But it is finding the pupa of the hive queen that gives Ender the greatest opportunity to achieve redemption. Not only does that discovery prove that he did not kill off the entire race of the formics, but it also gives him the chance to be the one who restores the race.

In fact, that mission to provide a new home for the formics is hinted at before he ever finds the pupa—even before he destroys their home world. While conducting the battles he thinks are simulations, at one point he pushes himself so hard that he makes himself sick. During that intense period, he has a dream that he dies and is buried: "Only a hill grew up where they laid his body down, and he dried out and became a home for buggers, like the Giant was."

That dream, it later turns out, was due to the formics' attempts to communicate with him telepathically through the ansible. Even as they realized that he would probably annihilate their world, the hive queens forgave Ender. And they built the fake body of the Giant on their colony world in order to lead Ender to the pupa. But the symbolism of Ender's body providing a home for formics clearly foreshadows the role the aliens hoped he would take on of finding the new hive queen a place to live and rebuild her race.

In Ender's mind, killing off an entire species is what Peter would do. Therefore, the chance to restore an extinct species to life is the final signifier that Ender is not like Peter. (The Speaker for the Dead persona gives Ender the opportunity to reconcile with Peter, and Ender realizes that his brother was not the monster he believed. But it is the childhood mental image of his brother, not his actual brother, that forms the standard against which he measures himself.) And although the actual restoration of the formics does not happen until later in the series, it is certainly implied by the final lines of this novel. Ender has found peace in his new purpose, and thus his emotional arc is complete.

—

Which brings us back to the question of how the novel should have ended. *Ender's Game* is not simply a story of an exceptional child who must outwit aliens in order to save the human race—it is the story of an exceptional child who fears he is a monster and is tricked into doing something monstrous.

By providing Ender with a way to redeem himself, *Ender's Game* ends exactly the way it should have ended.

*A Nebula Award winner, Hugo Award nominee, and winner in the Writers of the Future Contest, **Eric James Stone** has had stories published in* Year's Best SF 15, Analog, Nature, *and Kevin J. Anderson's* Blood Lite *anthologies of humorous horror, among*

other venues. Eric is also an assistant editor for Or-
son Scott Card's InterGalactic Medicine Show. His
short fiction collection, Rejiggering the Thingamajig
and Other Stories, *was published by Paper Golem
Press in 2011. Eric lives in Utah, and his website can
be found at www.ericjamesstone.com.*

Q. What do the IF tests measure?

A. If I knew the answer to this question, I'd make my fortune in educational testing! The whole idea of early-childhood testing depends on one true idea and one false one. The true idea is that children's character and capabilities manifest themselves very early in life, and the rest of their life is spent discovering, expanding on, or compensating for all the interests, talents, and handicaps that were present at the start.

The false idea is that an outsider is capable of knowing, or of designing any kind of test that would allow him to know, with certainty, which attributes will be important in forming a child's character. This is because initial aptitudes and proclivities, while they remain important throughout life, do not determine or even provide a hint at what the child will eventually *do* with or about those aptitudes and preferences.

So I don't believe such a test is possible. In fact, these tests are, in my opinion, the single most counterfactual element in the story of *Ender's Game*. But science fiction depends on making counterfactual assumptions and running with the results: What if people *could* design such early-childhood tests with a degree of success that could lead to the long-term existence of something like Battle School?'

Of course, the *failure* of such tests would not preclude their continued use; we have decades of experience with IQ and achievement tests, and many branches of pseudo-science or schools of thought within science, that prove people are able to hold on to provably absurd beliefs for an astonishingly long time, shaping public policy accordingly, and then refusing to admit the obvious consequences.

However, I was not writing a novel about how testing rarely shows what the testers believe that it shows. I posited instead that testing had actually become a science, and that the tests of these young children worked, at least well enough to bring some very, very talented children together in Battle School, with generally positive, useful results.

What would these fictional tests measure? They would have to include persistence at a task, aggressiveness, focus, anticipation of multiple consequences, envisioning of multiple alternative actions, formation of social bonds, perceptiveness about other people's motives, and successful prediction of other people's behavior. They would also test for verbal ability, logic, memory, and other standard IQ-test traits.

The use of monitors in addition to these tests is a tacit admission that even the best tests don't measure everything. Observation would be needed as well, and even then, the quality of the results of that observation would depend on the abilities of the people doing the observing.

—OSC

THE MONSTER'S HEART

JOHN BROWN

The moment we turn works of literature into puzzles, into clever and tricky essays that readers are supposed to sleuth through in order to find clues that reveal the true meaning—in that moment, the work dies. Oh sure, there are things to learn. But they are the things you learn from a cadaver, not the things you experience with a living soul.

For too long the discussion of literature has focused on meaning: on concepts, puzzles, symbols, themes, and ideas. On "what do you make of that?" I refuse to do that here with *Ender's Game*. I refuse to kill that story and everyone in it.

Why?

Because I prize the people I've met, the insights I've gleaned, the places I've been. I prize the experience. That's why I go to literature.

I don't watch *Fiddler on the Roof* about once every other year because of what it means. I don't watch the 1995 BBC production of *Pride and Prejudice* (the one starring Colin Firth) with my daughters with the same regularity because it's an exploration of views on women and class in the landed gentry of early-nineteenth-century England. I rewatch these stories because the people and situations in them delight me: they make me laugh, cry, and think. They change my heart.

I believe most readers go to fiction for the same reason. It's the experience we're after—the laughter, the delight, the poignancy, the loss, the longing, the triumph, the suspense, the insight. And so that's what I'm going to share with you here. I'll start by summarizing the process of literary experience and then discuss three parts of my joyful and poignant experience with Ender.

Snakes

A few years ago, my wife, four daughters, and I lived in a nine-hundred-square-foot home that my wife's grandmother had homesteaded up in the Rocky Mountains of northern Utah. It is made of rough-hewn logs that have been covered up with fading green aluminum siding on the outside and modern-day drywall inside. It has sloping floors, which means the oven slopes, resulting in cakes that are thick on one end and thin on the other. It also has one bathroom right off the kitchen with a trick door that will, now and again, open of its own accord, so that anyone sitting on the toilet can say hello to the visitors at the kitchen table (such a thoughtful door).

Because the house is in the mountains at the rural edge of the wilderness and a mile from the nearest neighbor, we had many wild visitors. Many in this area do. Moose, elk, eagles, badgers, rattlers, tourists wearing alarming summer wear—you name it; it's bound to show up in your yard eventually. For example, one of our neighbors was about to open her back door one day and saw a skunk hightailing it out of her yard. She wondered what was scaring it, then looked down at her dog's food bowl and saw two cougar kittens enjoying Fido's food, which is very cute until mamma cougar spots big-human-dinner and decides to drag it away by the neck.

At that time, my office was in a souped-up cow shed behind the house. One summer day, I came out of my shed, walked around the side of the house, and stepped on something slithering through the grass. Alarm immediately raced through me. I jerked back; my heart began to palpitate; I focused on the snake. It was long. Real long! It stretched at least twenty feet through the shaggy lawn. Then my reality meter went bong—a twenty-foot snake?!? I looked closer. It wasn't a snake—it was the garden hose! I laughed, my heart began to slow, and the adrenaline washed out of me. I continued on, probably to visit with said bathroom.

There are three parts to emotional experience as illustrated by that snake in the grass.

(1) Some sensory stimuli triggers a super-fast, rough, pre-cognitive appraisal that something in our environment is likely to affect our wants, interests, goals, values, etc., or those of someone we care about. In my case, my brain appraised that I'd stepped on a "bad slither." Fangs in your leg is kind of a big deal, especially when they may inject large

quantities of hemotoxic venom (yes, the kind that is real nifty for inducing heart failure).

(2) This pre-cognitive appraisal triggers physiological changes that help us focus attention on the situation, prepare us to respond, and communicate the situation to others. A lot of this physiological response is what we describe as emotion. For example, the feeling of romantic love is produced by a delightful cocktail of chemicals rushing to various parts of our bodies. The same goes for fear, rage, mirth, etc.

This physical response also affects subsequent appraisals. This occurs, in part, because of the focus I mentioned before, which is sometimes called the orienting reflex. When you see someone who may become the love of your life or someone intent on murdering you, it's helpful if you don't get distracted. The orienting reflex helps you keep your eye on both murderers and potential mates alike. However, if we're focusing on some things, that means we can't focus on or sometimes even see others. It also means new stimuli are fitted into the framework created by our initial appraisal.

For example, when you're alone in a dark house and already spooked, your physical response fixes your attention on threats. And so you will appraise the sound of something falling downstairs differently than when you're full of mirth or thinking about the fact that Johnny has been downstairs for a while and has been unusually quiet.

The effect of selective attention can be a great help—it filters out things that would otherwise be a distraction, at times when we can't afford to be distracted—but also can sometimes lead to damaging distortions. One of the central aspects of cognitive behavioral therapy when treating depression or phobia is to help the subject break out of the confines of their selective attention and see the details that lead them to appraise their situation in a more accurate manner.

With the snake, my brain focused, and ordered up some adrenaline and an increased heart rate to help me run; it also ordered up a flinch, and wrote *alarm* all over my face, which would draw the attention of others, who might help or flee.

(3) After the pre-cognitive appraisal and initial physiological response, which happens in less than the blink of an eye, we cognitively appraise the situation. This is the conscious thought part. In my case, I looked closer and thought, "It's a garden hose, you dope!" This new appraisal totally changed the nature of the situation. It triggered a different physiological response, including a new mix of emotion.

So we have these parts that feed into the process of emotion: cues in the environment, pre-cognitive appraisals of the situation, cognitive appraisals, and physiological responses. But what do these parts have to do with *Ender's Game*? Everything. Because we react in this way to more than sensory stimuli—we also react this way to our thoughts, including thoughts evoked by words on the page.

How is this possible?

It's possible because our pre-cognitive appraisals do not distinguish between real and imagined scenarios.[1] The pre-cognitive system takes whatever input is given—sensory or

---

[1] See Jenefer Robinson's marvelous *Deeper than Reason* for an introduction to emotion and literature. Then read the delightful *Thinking, Fast and Slow* by Daniel Kahneman to explore the ramifications of the two appraisal systems in a variety of other situations.

imagined—and appraises it. And that appraisal triggers the physical response.

This is why we can weep or laugh upon recalling some past event. We're not just remembering the event, we're reliving it, reappraising it. This is also why listening to a friend tell us a story about a terrible accident can make us cringe. Or listening to that same friend tell us about his toddler eating dog poo can make us cringe even harder. Even though we weren't present when the actual events occurred, we still witness the events in our minds, and our pre-cognitive system appraises them. This lack of distinction between sensory and imagined stimuli is why people with phobic fear of snakes not only fear real, live snakes but also have powerful reactions when simply imagining or reading about them.

You might think that our cognitive (conscious) appraisal system would come to the rescue with some reason. After all, didn't it point out that my snake was a garden hose? Won't it point out that our thoughts aren't real and, with regard to fiction, that the people and places we're reading about are all made up?

It can if something in the story is so unbelievable that our reality meters start to sound like mine did when I noticed the snake's length. But when the author presents plausible situations, our reality meters don't make a peep. They don't constantly remind us it's made up because our conscious thought is limited to the capacity of our working memory, and that capacity is small. Studies have shown that our working memory has room to hold only five to nine chunks of information at the same time. What constitutes a chunk can vary, but if you want to test this (as my fourteen-year-old did), have someone read you a list of ten to fourteen random names or numbers, then try to repeat those names or numbers back. You just can't hold more than five to nine things in your working memory at one time. But it gets worse. When we want to do anything with those chunks besides recall them (like manipulate them in a math problem or identify correlations between them), our capacity drops to two to four chunks.

Bottom line: our pipes for conscious thought aren't very fat. And so when what we're imagining completely maxes out that bandwidth, there is no room to think about the fact that it's just our imagination or just a work of fiction. We simply react to the imagined stimuli as if they were real and in front of us.

For fiction to provide an experience then, all it needs to do is present the situational cues to us that will automatically trigger our appraisals and physiological responses. This doesn't mean fiction must show us the situation. In fact, despite the often-repeated eleventh writing commandment, "Show, don't tell," the truth of the matter is that a text never shows a reader anything except marks on a page—it never presents the raw situational data through our senses. Movies and plays can show. They can also provide raw auditory input. But a book never *shows* us anything. It's *all* tell, tell, tell. The trick is to tell in a way that allows the reader to imagine the situation with enough clarity and realism that the imagined situation triggers the response. Of course, the situation itself (characters, motives, events, setting, etc.) needs to be ripe with potential in the first place, but developing that situation and helping the reader imagine it are two different things.

An author can guide a reader through a great variety of experiences—sympathy, suspense, poignancy, wonder, awe, mirth, dread, romantic love, etc. Orson Scott Card, in *Ender's Game*, guides us through a number of them. What I want to do now is explore part of that experience by doing what we all do when we quote lines from our favorite movies or books to each other: enjoy the experience all over again and, in the process, perhaps deepen it.

Transporting the Reader to Ender's World

When we read a book and feel as if we've been transported to another place, we often assume it's because the author has provided lots of setting detail. However, Card demonstrates that's not necessary. And, consequently, that what a writer is really doing is not "showing" but telling in a way that invites a reader to bring his or her own imagination to bear.

Let's look at the opening of *Ender's Game* as an example. We start off with two disembodied voices with zero setting nouns. As a result, I didn't see (imagine) any setting during that portion. But then we move into the scene where Ender's monitor is removed. That scene is 767 words long. How much of that is setting?

I'm sure you imagined it very clearly. I did. I saw (imagined) Ender in a doctor's office and a kind of operating room. It wasn't super-detailed, but I saw the examination table with white paper on it. I saw a male doctor, nurse, and another woman in white uniforms. I saw vague chrome shapes representing medical equipment surrounding them.

I saw a syringe. I saw bright light from overhead and more subdued lighting in the corners. I even felt a little cold.

But the text never mentions *uniforms* or *white*. It never mentions paper on the table or chrome. It never describes the syringe or the lighting. In fact, it says almost nothing. Card provides a whopping six setting nouns for his description: *monitor lady*, *horrible monitor*, *examining table*, *doctor*, *nurse*, *needle*.

Six.

And if you take away the characters, it's really only three.

What the...? How can he create a setting with just three general details?

It's possible because this is text and Card isn't *creating* a setting. He's helping us imagine one. He doesn't need to tell us about everything in detail for us to build the image in our minds. That wouldn't work anyway because of our working memory limitations. All he has to do is provide a few key words, and we pull up into working memory other constructs that we associate with those words.

This isn't a one-for-one relationship: Card's six descriptive terms won't prompt each reader to imagine exactly the same thing. For example, if you've never been in an operating room, there's no reason for you to have felt cold. And so I suspect what some of you imagined didn't include that. But I've been in plenty, and so that came with it. Of course, Card never said *operating room*, did he? He said *examination table*, which means this could be a warm room in a doctor's office. For whatever reason, I saw this as a more official procedure. You may have seen something slightly different.

But it really wouldn't have mattered, would it? Because the key thing Card is doing here is not transporting us to an exact place. It's transporting us to a character and a threat to his well-being. Who cares if you saw a small doctor's office and I saw an operating room? We both saw Ender almost become a vegetable. We both heard his interesting internal response to the statement that the removal wouldn't hurt a bit. We both learned that Ender's brother hated him, and that Ender just wanted not to be hated.

I'm not saying this is the optimal amount of setting stories should have. I'm simply saying that it doesn't take much to prompt a reader's mind to imagine a world. Furthermore, by limiting the time spent on setting, Card is able to spend more time helping the reader imagine the characters—their thoughts, motives, actions, and speech—and on the threats other characters pose to those we're rooting for. In movie terms, the vast majority of the scenes I imagined were simple medium and close-up shots, uncluttered by atmosphere. By nature, such shots are designed to focus on the characters. This focus is one of the hallmarks of Card's style—transporting us not so much to the place as the mind and heart.

Card's decision to focus on character over setting isn't simply a stylistic *choice du jour*. If you think about novels as the result of authors finding and inventing cool things to share with readers, then it's clear that Card delights in sharing the inner workings of his characters. He delights in sharing motives and reactions that are not always what's expected at first blush. Or as simple.

Stage time is precious, and Card spends a huge portion of his telling us why Ender does what he does. He also transports us to the motives of others. The disembodied voices at the beginning of each chapter discuss their motives. Valentine constantly guesses at Peter's motives. Ender constantly appraises why the people around him do what they do. His special insight is one of his larger-than-life gifts. For example, it's not enough to know that Bonzo Madrid feels compelled to attack Ender because Ender undercut him. Ender digs deeper, appraising how his culture and role as commander of the Salamander Army plays into the situation.

But it's not just the characters that are appraising the situations they face. Card is guiding us in our appraisals of those same situations. Sometimes our appraisal matches the character's. Sometimes we have privileged information that leads to a different view. And sometimes it's the character who has surprising special insight that alters our perceptions. Card likes to dig below the surface, and this allows him to guide us into a series of appraisals that sometimes change our response as dramatically as my response was changed when I realized what I'd stepped on was a hose, not a snake.

The Hive Queen: From Revulsion to Love

The crowning scene of *Ender's Game*, its last gift, is all about going beyond the surface to know why someone does a thing and how knowing the *why* can completely change our appraisal of that person. Ender becomes the Speaker for the Dead, but it's in the scene with the hive queen that the reader experiences what such a *speaking* means.

Through most of the story, our knowledge of the formics is limited. We know that they look like bugs, don't communicate with us, and slaughter us without provocation or remorse. It's us or this plague of horrible insects. But at the end, after Ender has destroyed the formics and gone to live on another planet, he finds the playground the formic queen built for him. He finds the egg. And we are guided into an experience that alters our view of the formics forever. In this scene, Card presents to us a snake, and then transforms it into something entirely different.

Ender describes the egg and the mating, the males shuddering in ecstasy and dying, dropping to the floor to shrivel. It's a bit disgusting, like something you might see in one of those uncouth nature programs. And, having witnessed the mating, our pre-cognitive appraisal leads to the same response we have when watching the nature programs—ick! Our first experience with the formics tags them as alien and repulsive. Clearly not one of us.

But then our view of them starts to change. Instead of focusing on things insectly grotesque, we are told to imagine the queen as majestic, clothed in shimmering wings. Then we're told she "kisses" her child, her daughter. Card then has us imagine her realization that all her children were going to die in the attack of the third wave, and that she was unable to do anything to avoid it. Notice that he prompts us to imagine her offspring as "children," not insects.

Then Card takes this all another step further. "They did not forgive us," the hive queen says. "We will surely die." We imagine a mother who feels enough remorse to want forgiveness.

We respond in sympathy to others when we see (1) a basically good, deserving person (2) suffering some form of hardship. Card has led us to imagine things that not only anthropomorphize the queen and her children but also show her goodness and hardship. In the space of a few lines, I was suddenly appraising things from her point of view. Did you not feel the same change as you read?

We're next guided to imagine the strange requirements for the hatching of the egg and a "small and fragile queen" emerging from it. And even though the hatching clearly reminds us that the hive queen is other, nothing here is grotesque. Furthermore, we are led directly into imagining the grief the queen feels at killing the humans. We know finally why the formics didn't come in another wave—they "did not mean to murder." They didn't even know, couldn't imagine, that we were thinking beings. We were bugs to them. Their final desperate cry rings in our ears: "Believe us, believe us, believe us." Please don't kill my last child, our last sister.

Card has led us from imagining the antecedents that trigger fear and revulsion to imagining those that completely reverse our appraisal. And we respond accordingly. By this point, I had tears in my eyes. I had sympathy for the helpless babe and the sorrowing mother as she faces death, trying to give her child a chance. I felt an anxious desire for the humans to hear their cry, which was "our" cry because I was on their side. The formics were good "people" who meant no harm, who had simply made a terrible mistake. The same one, in fact, that the humans make: Ender is as much the monster to them as they are to us. Then Ender writes his book, and the hive queen speaks with such forgiveness and magnanimity, it's impossible not to be slightly in awe of her goodness. She is different, but she is one of the best of us.

The loss, the poignancy, the sympathy for this supposed enemy—all of that is added into the experience of the book so that it's not just an adventure; it's not just a story about space or how to lead; it's not just about military games or trying to survive bullies and psychopaths who are trying to kill you. It's also about "making us human in each other's eyes." And Card doesn't just tell us that—he guides us so that it goes down into our bones, so that it's not just an idea but is stamped in our hearts.

The Silence of Peter's Speaking

One might think we would feel this same sympathy for Peter, whom, we are told, Ender speaks for as well. But Card does not present any of the content, and so we do not experience a change of heart like we did for the hive queen. It's true that Valentine tells Ender at the lake in chapter thirteen that "Peter's changed." But the fact is that I was never led to imagine what was necessary to feel or believe it.

What was I led to imagine instead?

We start in chapter one knowing that Peter hates Ender for having the monitor longer than he did. Then in chapter two we are led through one of the most frightening scenes of the book. Peter threatens Ender into playing formics and astronauts and in short order has him on his back and begins to suffocate him. Ender thinks Peter might not mean to kill him, might simply be trying to hurt him like he has in the past, but Peter, reading his mind, tells him, "I do mean it. Whatever you think, I mean it." Only Valentine's quick thinking saves Ender.

There was no doubt in my mind Peter wanted to kill Ender. I'd already been primed with Stilson to see what people in this culture thought about Thirds. And even though Peter relents when he sees he can't get away with murder at this time, he vows to kill Ender by lulling both him and Valentine into a false sense of security. My anxiety for Ender at that point was extremely high. Ender then explicitly tells us how to appraise the situation so we make no mistake. Peter may fool the adults, but "Peter was a murderer at heart, and nobody knew it but Valentine and Ender."

What a first impression. Yes, Peter comes into Ender's room later that night (Ender thinking maybe Peter has come to kill him) and tells Ender he's sorry, that he loves him. But isn't that what Peter promised to do —lull Ender into believing he won't kill him?

We see Peter next in chapter nine. It opens with the voices of those who monitored the thoughts of Peter, telling us "he's one of the worst human beings we've laid hands on." This is the judgment of those who supposedly know Peter inside and out. We are not led to imagine anything that would contradict this appraisal, so there's no reason to question them.

Valentine tells us that the Wiggins move to North Carolina, hoping nature will soften Peter. She says that Peter has fooled all the adults, but she knows different. Then she describes the squirrels Peter flays alive. She suspects this was a way for Peter to satisfy his need to kill, but the first words out of Peter's mouth when he comes onstage again show us he's as dangerous as ever. He says to Valentine, "I've been deciding whether to kill you or what."

And I believe him. I feel danger every time that boy comes onstage. And why shouldn't I? To this point, we haven't been led to imagine anything that would lead to any other response.

Peter explains he wants her help. He doesn't want to destroy anyone. He admits he was cruel. He says he loved both her and Ender and that it was all because "I just had to be—had to have control, do you understand that?" He tells her control is the most important thing for him. It's his gift to see the weak points in things. And now he wants to "save mankind from self-destruction."

But Valentine doesn't buy it. She confronts him about killing the squirrels, saying, "You did it because you love to do it." Peter weeps. "It's what I'm most afraid of," he says. "That I really am a monster. I don't want to be a killer but I just can't help it." Valentine thinks while he might be telling the truth, it's only to manipulate her. Then he asks her to be his partner in everything so she can keep him from becoming "like the bad ones."

Here's our chance to revise our appraisal of Peter, but he's so full of lies and manipulation we can't trust it. Any hopes we might have had for him are discarded a few pages later when Valentine is asked if Peter is a bad person, and she responds by saying he's "the worst person I know." Indeed, he's the worst we know in the book as well.

In chapter thirteen, when we return to Valentine's point of view, the voices at the beginning of the chapter reaffirm that Peter "has the soul of a jackal." Furthermore, Valentine tells us that Peter still frightens her. She tells Ender he's changed, but we're given nothing that would help us imagine another person. Time after time after time, we are only led to imagine a psychopath.

At the end of the lake chapter, Graff and Ender discuss the fact that they can't communicate with the formics. Graff concludes, "If the other fellow can't tell you his story, you can never be sure he isn't trying to kill you." Perhaps Peter *has* told us his story; perhaps what he says to Valentine is an accurate reflection of his thoughts. But it's clear we need more to trust the story is true. We need more to even understand what Peter's need for control means. In the end, Card never guides us into imagining anything that would allow us to trust Peter. And so all we can conclude is that Peter has some new scheme, one that doesn't require he murder Valentine, yet.

From start to finish, Peter triggers nothing but loathing and fear.

The *Why* Matters

Throughout the story, Ender fears he'll become a monster, a murderer like Peter. But as a reader, I could not share that fear because any action someone might take is only part of what we use to appraise the morality of a situation. The other part is revealed in chapter three when Ender's mother sarcastically asks Colonel Graff if he'd have given Ender a medal if he'd killed Stilson. Graff replies, "It isn't what he did, Mrs. Wiggin. It's why."

Indeed, if there's anything the experience of *Ender's Game* teaches us, it's that the *why* matters. Peter is a monster not because he does things that cause others pain but because of the *why* behind them. He is only motivated by a desire to control. The hive queen slaughtered great numbers of humans, but the why of her actions transforms that act from evil to tragic ignorance. In all his altercations with Stilson, Peter, Bernard, and Bonzo, Ender only fights to secure his safety. He kills two boys and wipes out a whole species, but we don't condemn him for it because he is never acting to hurt someone else, only to defend. And so we end up rooting for him instead.

The *why* is a vital part of our appraisal of any situation and, therefore, has a direct effect on our response.

Although Peter can only see people as tools in his schemes, Ender is filled with a desire to be kind. In fact, in the surprising discussion with Valentine at the lake, Ender reveals to her that he doesn't want to beat Peter. He only wants Peter to love him. Someone might read that as Stockholm syndrome, except we've been given Ender's mind and heart, and there's no evidence of that. Ultimately, Ender goes back to fight the formics to save Valentine, the one who loved him, who was his anchor, "even if she loved Peter more."

My eyes stung and my heart swelled when Ender revealed he thought Valentine loved Peter more. This is not the heart of a monster. Ender, who can read the motives of others so well, can't seem to see the difference between Peter's motives and his own. Nor is he able to see clearly, in this instance, the motives of Valentine, the one who loves him so very much. Ender never needed to fear he was becoming Peter.

On the other hand, perhaps the quality of his heart is precisely what led him to worry. Perhaps that is part of what defines who is a good guy and who is not—the good guys realize they are as corruptible as any, and so they watch themselves, making sure both their actions and motives are as right as they can make them.

Peter Revisited

Did you notice the progression of appraisals I made above? Card presented the scene that triggered my initial tears for Ender. And then my cognitive appraisals kicked in, modifying my response, making it even more complex. Yes, it's sad Ender can't see he's not like Peter at all, nor how much Valentine loves him. But upon reflection, the new thought and cognitive appraisal about what motivates "good guys" adds admiration to that sadness and transforms it into a more poignant experience. It also demonstrates something else.

Ender's Game guides us through many moments of science fictional awe, fearful suspense, and triumph. A number of these experiences depend on Card guiding us into surprising appraisals of the situations we witness—appraisals that focus not on the externals but on the motives of the characters we meet. But it's not only what Card has us imagine that forms our experience. It's also what we imagine ourselves. We add our own imaginings to what Card presents us in the text and react to them with just as much power.

For example, the second time I read the last battle between the humans and the formics, I knew it wasn't just a game but real humans sacrificing themselves. A brief image flickered into my mind of a group of people on a bridge in one of those ships looking at each other just before the end.

My heart swelled, and my experience of *Ender's Game* was changed and deepened yet again. Truly, the experience of a book isn't a fixed thing but something that changes over time. And changes outside the text.

Another even more poignant change came after I closed the book and began to develop my ideas for the very essay you're reading. Going back through all my experiences with Peter, I suddenly had another thought and cognitive appraisal. Despite all the awful things we see him do, one might argue that Peter is the greatest hero of this book because he struggles against greater obstacles than anyone else—his psychopathy is in his DNA. He can't help but want to kill, and yet he uses his hurtful instincts to work for world peace.

Is it possible? Did Peter have a heart that could love? We are never led, in the book, to imagine the antecedents that would trigger that assessment. It is only by adding my own imagination—a flash of a little boy struggling in dismay—and subsequent cognitive appraisals that I can feel deep sympathy for his plight as well as a mixture of awe and admiration at his struggle.

Did Card show us the hearts of three monsters, and show them all to be good? Could Peter actually be a hero?

I don't know. I truly don't.

But that thought, that prick of sympathy for that terrible boy, struggling against huge odds to do what's right, is now part of my *Ender's Game* experience.

Ultimately, even if Peter isn't a hero, my time with Ender led me to think at least about the possibility. And perhaps, of all the wonderful gifts *Ender's Game* has to give, this might be one of the finest. To help me remember—through hours of thrilling, heartbreaking, and ultimately triumphant experience—that although there are indeed a variety of monsters in life that must be dealt with, not all are necessarily what they seem. And to help me, if only a little, yearn for a more Ender-, and perhaps Peter-, and hive queen–like heart.

John Brown is an award-winning novelist and short story writer. Servant of a Dark God is the first in his epic fantasy series published by Tor Books. Brown currently lives with his wife and four daughters in the hinterlands of Utah, where one encounters much fresh air, many good-hearted ranchers, and an occasional wolf.

Q. Why is Ender ashamed of being a Third?

A. Ender learned early in life that he was taunted by some kids, and resented or shunned by others, because he was a third child. Long before he understood the legal restrictions on family size, he knew that it was socially unacceptable to be a third child. Later, he would learn that his birth came about because of reasons that redounded positively on his siblings and that his existence was neither illegal nor shameful, but it's very hard to overcome the visceral experience of community rejection that he underwent from earliest childhood.

—OSC

Q. Is the Wiggin predisposition to military genius a natural genetic one, or was it altered in some artificial way?

When authorizing Ender to be born, did the IF use genetic manipulation or genetic screening, assuming they were choosing from a pool of zygotes? How could the IF be sure that Ender would be the perfect mix of Peter and Valentine?

A. The IF was not sure Ender would work out well. Peter and Valentine came so close, and were so off-the-charts excellent on some vital measures, that the IF thought the odds were very good that a third child from the same parents would be suitable for command.

The only genetic manipulation was that the IF suggested Ender's parents time the conception in ways that increase the prevalence of Y rather than X spermatozoa, because a male child would be more likely to have the aggressiveness that Valentine lacked.

—OSC

Q. How was Peter too cruel or crazy to not be allowed into Battle School? Isn't that what the military wanted, a person that would utterly destroy the formics? I believe that Peter would have destroyed them with the Little Doctor without hesitating or regretting it, like Ender.

A. It isn't enough to be eager to defeat the enemy. You also have to be able to inspire the loyalty, trust, and obedience of underlings and superiors within your own organization. As the Shadow books chronicle, Peter spent much of his life trying to learn things that came naturally to Ender, in order to be able to inspire people to follow his leadership politically. He would not have been able to do so within the time limits already looming over the project.

Soldiers will not willingly follow a commander who is so gung-ho that they believe he does not care about their well-being. It was Ender's palpable love and concern for other soldiers, training them as assiduously as he trained himself, that inspired love and loyalty. Peter wouldn't even have thought of behaving toward other soldiers as Ender did.

—*OSC*

THE COST OF BREAKING THE RULES

MARY ROBINETTE KOWAL

I n 2005, I was fortunate enough to attend Orson Scott Card's Literary Boot Camp. I had read his books *Characters and Viewpoint* and *How to Write Science Fiction and Fantasy*, but his boot camp itself was a transformative experience. Before boot camp, I felt as though I could write a good story by accident, and afterward, as though I could write one on purpose.

Card explained the rules and how fiction worked so clearly that it had gone from being a mysterious process to being something repeatable. After the camp, I pulled out my battered copy of *Ender's Game* and re-read it because I wanted to see how he applied the rules that he just taught us.

I was stunned. Card breaks the rules all over the place. Pretty much every piece of wisdom I'd received in his boot camp, he took and inverted at least once in the book. One of the things he told us on Day One was, "If you catch yourself being wise, put it into the mouth of a fool." But on the second page, he gives Ender, who is anything but a fool, this bit of wisdom:

> It was a lie, of course, that it wouldn't hurt a bit. But since adults always said it when it was going to hurt, he could count on that statement as an accurate prediction of the future. Sometimes lies were more dependable than the truth.

Card *has* to establish Ender as being really smart, so he has to give him moments of wisdom that are beyond his years. And that's just the beginning of the rule-breaking. What I eventually realized, though, was that when Card broke the rules, it was for a reason that served the story.

In many ways, what Card *really* teaches in his classes is the same lesson that Ender eventually learns in Battle School: there are no rules. The first time Ender breaks a rule is when Bonzo tells him not to fire a shot during battles. Ender follows the rule at first, and then one day, he steps through the gate and saves the army from total defeat by firing. He waited to break the rule until the cost of following the rule was higher than that of ignoring it.

In fact, during class, Card had even said, "You can break any of the rules as long as you understand the cost." Even though I dutifully wrote that down in the notes I took, it wasn't until I saw that principle at work in *Ender's Game* that I understood how much freedom a writer has. Or that, with that freedom, comes a responsibility to the reader. If a writer is going to break the rules, he has to do it with deliberate intention and an understanding of the effect.

In my journal, when the camp ended, I wrote "that it was as if someone had taken off the top of my head and said, 'You don't have to stop here.'"

What I want to show you is all the ways that Card subverts the rules in *Ender's Game*, and what he gains by doing it.

"Avoid starting with unattributed dialogue" (Orson Scott Card, 2005 Literary Boot Camp)

At the start of a story, the reader has to build the world based on the information the author provides. This makes the order in which the author unveils information very, very important. Starting with unattributed dialogue means that readers have to work harder to understand what is happening. They don't know the setting or who is speaking. Heck, they don't even know the gender of the character. In reality, it is a very rare instance in which one would know nothing about the environment before hearing someone speak. Even in a dark room, it's almost always possible to tell the gender of the person speaking.

With a line of unattributed dialogue, readers are at sea. What winds up happening is that readers will see the dialogue and then have to re-read and re-process it once they know where the story is set and who is speaking. It's presenting the information backwards and is an extra step that slows down readers' engagement with the story. The simplest example is when a reader thinks that a character is one gender and then finds out that the character is the other. More complex and less predictable are readers' assumptions about a character's emotional state. Take the sentence: "What did you say?" Without context, that could be an angry parent, a confused child, or a girl in a dive bar. Card taught us to give that context right up front so that we could control our readers' perceptions and guide them through the story.

And yet.

I know you've read it, but just flip open to the first page of *Ender's Game*. Card started the novel not just with a *line* of unattributed dialogue but an entire half-page of it.

There is no setting. There are no dialogue tags. He tells us *nothing* about the people who are speaking. It's more like an unattributed transcript than anything else.

This does make the reader work harder to figure out who the speakers are and what they are talking about, but because we can see that section is so short, it also acts to pique our curiosity. He turned the weaknesses of starting with dialogue into a strength but is able to do so, I think, only because he has a firm understanding of the effect it has on a reader.

It tells us that the story is *not* about the people who are speaking. If this scene started in a tight third-person point of view, we would start to get emotionally invested in the characters. By having us eavesdrop, in essence, by denying them names, a location, or even genders, Card is able to focus our attention on the subject of their conversation and away from them. Who *is* this kid they are talking about? It makes us want to know more about him, and then Card immediately follows up by giving us a scene from Ender's point of view.

Because he answers the question of *Who are they talking about?* right away, it builds audience trust that he will answer the other questions, such as *Who is speaking?*, *What is important about this kid?*, and *What are the buggers?*

So, although this looks like a violation of a principle that Scott teaches, it is actually adhering to the other, more important one: you can do anything, as long as you understand the cost.

In this case, Card was paying the cost of some disconnection with his audience in exchange for a heightened tension. It's not a trick that can be used often, but it worked very well here.

"Trading viewpoints requires a clear division—a chapter break or line space. The limited third-person narrator can never change viewpoints in mid-scene." (Orson Scott Card, *Characters and Viewpoint*)

Among writers in the science fiction community, this is almost a mantra that we repeat to new writers. It's such a common beginner's mistake to jump around in viewpoint that it actually has a shorthand name: head-hopping, called that because of the sensation of hopping from one person's head to another. It is jarring for a reader suddenly to get thoughts from someone else.

Most of *Ender's Game* is written in limited third-person narration. However, Card breaks rules with point of view in a couple of places. The most interesting of these—or to put it more accurately, the one that made my head explode with wonder—is in chapter twelve.

Card starts the scene in Ender's point of view, then he changes viewpoint characters to Bean, at mid-chapter, with no line breaks. This should be a flaw, but watch what he does.

Ender shook his head. "All I know is, the game's over." He folded up the paper. "None too soon. Can I tell my army?"

"There isn't time," said Graff. "Your shuttle leaves us in twenty minutes. Besides, it's better not to talk to them after you get your orders. It makes it easier."

"For them or for you?" Ender asked. He didn't wait for an answer. He turned quickly to Bean, took his hand for a moment, and then headed for the door.

"Wait," said Bean. "Where are you going? Tactical? Navigational? Support?"

"Command School," Ender answered.

"*Pre*-command?"

"Command," said Ender, and then he was out of the door. Anderson followed him closely. Bean grabbed Colonel Graff by the sleeve. "Nobody goes to Command School until they're sixteen!"

Graff shook off Bean's hand and left, closing the door behind him.

Bean stood alone in the room, trying to grasp what this might mean.

See? He uses the *action* of the scene, in which Ender is ushered out of the room, to manage the transition. The camera, as it were, stays in the room and remains focused on Bean. It is a very simple trick, in which he directs the reader's attention through the narrative. For Ender, the scene is over dramatically. His next several hours are going to be spent traveling. If Card had followed him, then the tension would have dropped off. Bean, on the other hand, still has questions and can maintain the dramatic tension that Card worked so hard to build. If he had followed convention and had a line break there, it would have interrupted the momentum of the scene. In this case, adhering to standard practice would have exacted a greater cost than playing with the rules. By breaking them, Card keeps the tension high and the reader engaged.

"Don't violate the time-flow of the story" (Orson Scott Card, 2005 Literary Boot Camp)

The idea here is that humans experience time in a linear fashion, so stories that follow a straight time-flow are easier to grasp. They feel more natural because they meet the readers' expectations of how time works. It feels like the narrative is unfolding as though it were real life. Within that, a flashback is a recognized technique that mimics the way memory works.

There's another thing that might be called a flashforward. It's when the narration says something like, "At the time, he didn't understand. Later, he realized that…" Usually it jars readers out of a story, even if it is on an unconscious level, by reminding them that this is a story. It's not just that it points out the presence of the narrator, but it reduces the tension by suggesting that the events being described had happened in the past.

In chapter four, Card violates the time-flow.

> He imagined the ship dangling upside down on
> the undersurface of the Earth, the giant fingers of
> gravity holding them firmly in place. But we will
> slip away, he thought. We are going to fall off this
> planet.
>   He did not know its significance at the time.
> Later, though, he would remember that it was even
> before he left Earth that he first thought of it as a
> planet, like any other, not particularly his own.

When Card pulls the stunt of "Later, he would remember…," it comes at a cost. It reminds us that this is a narrative. That price buys him something, though.

It makes us pay attention to this moment by adding significance to it. If Ender is going to remember this moment later, then the reader should as well. Most of the time, with something that you want the character and reader to remember later, you expand the moment and have it play out longer. You make it more emotionally significant, in the moment, to the character, and then you drop reminders of it later. Here, it's not an emotionally important moment to Ender. It's just a game that he is playing with his imagination and understanding of gravity. Trying to expand the scene wouldn't work here because it would slow the pacing down and delay the moment when we arrive at Battle School. Again, this is a place where Card turns a weakness into a strength. He uses the narrator to point at something that is insignificant to Ender *in that moment* but *is* significant to the overall narrative. Does he remind us that we're reading a story? Yes. But that consciousness is what cements the moment in our mind.

Again, in chapter fourteen, Card pulls what appears to be the same trick and violates the time-flow.

> The next day was his last day in Command School,
> though he didn't know it.

In this case, the thing he's buying is not the implantation of a memory. This time, when he breaks that rule, he is asking the reader to pay more attention. It's like saying, "This scene I'm about to show you? It's not going to go down the way you think it is. Pay attention." It reminds the reader that a narrator is there. It's almost a dare, like he's telling us to go ahead and try to guess what will happen next.

The challenge is that if the pay-off isn't as cool as the reader's guess, the author risks losing the reader completely. At the same time, that break seems necessary here.

All through chapter fourteen, we've been in Ender's head, and he's seriously dazed with exhaustion. It's easy to drift into a fugue state with him. That moment of violating the time-flow snaps a reader out of it. It comes at a cost, but the cost of reminding us that this is a story is very much worth the dramatic tension it buys.

"Don't make aliens that are just like [x] but smart" (Orson Scott Card, 2005 Literary Boot Camp)

Card isn't the only one who teaches this these days. It's the sort of rule that makes sense because, if aliens evolved on another planet, why would they have anything in common with life on Earth? In his book, *How to Write Science Fiction and Fantasy*, he also says: "I always start the alien-building part of the session by asking, 'How do these aliens differ from human beings?' I reject the obvious similes. 'They're like cats.' 'They're like dogs.' I insist on something truly strange."

But in the same book, Card talks about how he took this rule and deliberately broke it when he created the formics. "Who was the enemy they were training to fight? Other humans? No, aliens—cliché aliens at that. Bug-eyed monsters. Our worst nightmares, only now they were here in real life."

It's interesting to examine the way in which he took that cliché of the giant insect and made a believable society for it. So let's look at how he got the readers to buy it.

He does this in layers. In the second chapter, Peter and Ender play astronauts and buggers, complete with a rubber mask. This is actually a fairly meta-moment, when you think about it. Card created aliens based on the cliché of the bug-eyed rubber mask aliens of film and television, then hangs a flag on it by having a scene with an actual rubber mask. It allows him to acknowledge the cliché and then move on.

By also making it a children's game, it eases the reader into the idea of what the formics are rather than confronting them with the idea of bug-eyed monsters right up front. Children simplify things, so the reader can still think that, although the formics might have bug-like characteristics, they won't turn out to be actual bugs.

As the book progresses, though, we get comfortable thinking about the formics as bugs, just the way everyone else in the Enderverse does.

By the time we get to chapter fourteen, we've bought into the idea of the formics as giant bugs. So we are ready for the last layer.

Mazer Rackham says, "And something else. Something so childish and stupid that the xenobiologists laughed me to silence when I said it after the battle. The buggers are *bugs.* They're like ants and bees. A queen, the workers."

Again, this is hanging a flag on something that ought to be a weakness. Mazer tells us, flat out, that this is a stupid idea. But Card has spent the entire book telling us how incredibly smart Mazer Rackham is, so at this moment, when he says the idea is stupid, we know that it's not.

We have, at this point, completely bought into the idea of giant insects.

"Dreams have no author. In stories they are a cheap way to add sub-text" (Orson Scott Card, 2005 Literary Boot Camp)

A real dream is a random collection of images. Your brain stitches the images together to have meaning after the fact, but real dreams are never as tidy as they are in fiction. Many beginning authors will use dreams as a way to shed some light on the interior landscape of a character, rather than doing the work of carrying that character's emotional baggage through into their waking life. It falls flat with readers because waking and dreaming don't mirror each other so precisely.

In *Ender's Game*, there are a long string of nightmares and dreams that plague Ender, culminating in a series of them in chapter fourteen after Ender has been pushed through battle after battle in Command School. He is clearly breaking down, and he dreams of Valentine, Peter, and of being vivisected by formics. Card makes these dreams work by employing two different tricks. In the first case, Ender thinks he is dreaming but is not.

> In his dream, the voices sounded like Colonel Graff and Mazer Rackham. But that was the way dreams were, the craziest things could happen, because he dreamed he heard one of the voices saying, "I can't bear to see what this is doing to him." And the other voice answered, "I know. I love him too."

Because of the other scenes with Colonel Graff, we know that this is something that he would actually say. It is easy to believe the same of Mazer Rackham, so as a reader, we know that Ender is not dreaming.

But Card goes one step further and hangs a flag on the unnaturalness of dreams in literature when the narration says, "That was the way dreams were, the craziest things could happen." By acknowledging that dreams are inherently disjointed and random, he lets the reader know that showing us a coherent dream is an intentional choice. It is the authorial equivalent of saying, "I know this sounds crazy, but trust me."

He needs that trust because he then pushes the envelope of what dreams can do even further with the second of the two tricks I mentioned.

But in the night he thought of other things. Often he remembered the corpse of the Giant, decaying steadily; he did not remember it, though, in the pixels of the picture on his desk. Instead it was real, the faint odor of death still lingering near it. Things were changed in his dreams. The little village that had grown up between the Giant's ribs was composed of buggers now, and they saluted him gravely, like gladiators greeting Caesar before they died for his entertainment. He did not hate the buggers in his dream; and even though he knew that they had hidden their queen from him, he did not try to search for her.

Clearly, this is too coherent to be an actual dream. If it came early in the novel, most readers would think, "Oh please," because the dream is so thematically laden. I can almost picture the Battle School psych experts discussing the way the dream *perfectly* captures Ender's anxiety about destroying his attackers completely and his ongoing desire to be forgiven for their deaths. Early in the book, something this heavy-handed would seem like "a cheap way to add sub-text." By coming so late in the book, Card has bought our trust. Even so, there's a risk to such a clear dream. The author risks throwing the reader out of the story just for a moment before they decide to believe that Ender's brain delivered such nice sub-text to him by chance.

Having read the book, you know that the key lies on the next page. Here, again, Card hangs a flag on the dreams: "It was as if someone rode him in his sleep, forcing him to wander through his worst memories, to live in them again as if they were real."

He basically comes right out and says, "These aren't just dreams. Wait for it."

When we do, the pay-off is there. The formics, who communicate instantly, of course rifle through Ender's brain. It makes so much sense.

To do that, though, Card had to have already gained our trust by always following through earlier in the novel on the implicit promises in the narrative. Remember that first set of questions he set up for us on the first page? That was the opening move in a long negotiation to buy our trust. Trying to use this trick in a story without aliens like the formics wouldn't work because you need their sheer alien-ness, to create the necessity for such communication, and their ability to connect directly, mind to mind. Even trying to do this earlier in the novel would not have worked because it would have meant asking the reader to believe actively that the dreams are plausible, and some readers, not yet fully invested in the story, might not be willing to suspend their disbelief. It's a tricky balance but worth the cost in the end.

All of these rules that Card breaks are things that it makes sense to teach new writers while they are getting the hang of fiction. The thing that I stress now, when I teach, is that these are principles or guidelines, not rules. People think they have to follow the rules religiously. Or they see an example like *Ender's Game*, where the rules are broken and think that none of them matter.

But as Ender says, "Everyone had learned the wrong lesson."

The rules *do* matter. They help the reader make sense of the story. The challenge is to understand the cost. Just like for Ender, sometimes there's a cost for following the rules that is higher than for breaking them.

Mary Robinette Kowal *is the author of* Shades of Milk and Honey *(Tor, 2010) and* Glamour in Glass *(Tor, 2012). In 2008 she received the Campbell Award for Best New Writer, and in 2011 her short story "For Want of a Nail" won the Hugo Award for Short Story. Her work has been nominated for the Hugo, Nebula, and Locus awards. Her stories appear in Asimov's, Clarkesworld, and several Year's Best anthologies. Mary, a professional puppeteer, also performs as a voice actor, recording fiction for authors such as Seanan McGuire, Cory Doctorow, and John Scalzi. She lives in Chicago with her husband, Rob, and over a dozen manual typewriters. Visit www. maryrobinettekowal.com.*

Q. How come you shut out any kind of relationship with Ender and his parents? It seemed to me that there should have been some kind of stronger bond. If I were a parent I would want to see my son, and not just send Val to talk to him. Or towards the end, after the war, why didn't you have him come home to Earth for at least a week to say his goodbyes before making him an outcast?

A. You're really asking three questions here:

1. Why did I, as a writer, avoid developing a relationship between Ender and his parents?
2. Why did the Battle School cut the children off completely from their parents?
3. Why did Ender's parents accept the situation?

I'll answer these in reverse order.

Why did Ender's parents accept the situation?

Ender's parents were allowed—no, encouraged—to have a third child *only* if they accepted the terms from the International Fleet (and therefore the Hegemony government). Ender would have to wear the brain-linked monitor from infancy on; if Ender was selected for

Battle School, then he would be taken from them, period. They would lose all parental rights from then on.

They grieved when Ender was taken from them, but they had understood from before his birth that this was possible, even likely, and that if and when the time came, there would be no appeal and no recourse. In such circumstances, when parents know that they cannot keep a child, they simultaneously cling to every moment together *and* begin the process of separation and farewell. Of course, the degree to which they cling or separate depends on their individual characters.

Ender's parents were brilliant, tough people—and both were more analytical than passionate in their actions and expressions. They felt as much as anyone, but did not act on, or act out, their feelings to the degree that many others might have. To outside observers, this might make it seem that they felt little, but this is not true. People often keep their grief utterly private; it does not mean they feel less, only that they show less.

At the end of the war, their failure to send for Ender and communicate with him hurt Ender greatly (as depicted in *Ender in Exile*). But by that time, years had passed. They did not feel that they knew Ender. They did not want to intrude on his new life. So they were waiting for some kind of invitation from him, some signal that he would welcome contact from them. This was a mistake—he was, after all, still a child. But from their perspective, he was the "child" who had saved the world; he was now so famous, so important, that they might be forgiven for feeling that he was out of reach to them, that he was now in the superior power position, and that it was up to him to make the first move.

He was no longer the Ender Wiggin that they knew—the precocious six-year-old who was taken away from them. He was a stranger, a creature of Battle School, a boy who had conquered an alien species; he was Alexander the Great. What were they going to do, bring him home and help him through junior high school?

This is not to say that their actions were right, only that they were not inhumane. When Ender Wiggin was taken away, it was with the understanding that he would not belong to them anymore; he was from then on a child of the International Fleet.

Why did the Battle School cut the children off completely from their parents?

The Battle School was the ultimate boarding school. At the beginning, they did allow contact between parents and children. But after visits, the children's performance suffered greatly. They were less attentive in school; their progress lagged; they were more likely to be rebellious; and they were definitely more unhappy.

At first, most kids were homesick and longed for home and parents, but after a year or two, their feelings reversed. Most students wanted to stop visiting with their parents; most of them didn't even want their parents' letters. They had nothing to say to their parents—how could their families understand about life in Battle School? And the children were completely uninterested in what was going on at home. That life was over for them. Their identification was complete.

Remember that these children were selected because they were exactly right for Battle School. They responded positively to their training regimen and to the culture of Battle School, which was designed not to break their spirit, but to enliven their instinct for command and competition. Nothing at home could compare to the near-perfection of this culture. If they were not the kind of child who would thrive in Battle School, they were not brought there.

So the administrators of Battle School discovered the following pattern: At first, homesick children would write to their parents begging to see them, to come home again, which made the parents frantic with worry. But then, after a year or two, the letters from their children became perfunctory and then stopped altogether. The parents became even *more* worried; thinking that the children still felt as homesick as they had before, they thought the school was stopping them from writing. And when the parents finally realized their children really didn't *want* to visit or call or write any more, it was devastating.

But once the school instituted the zero-contact policy, everything went better. The parents did not expect to be able to see or communicate with their children. And while the children were allowed to write, venting their initial homesickness, the letters were never delivered, so the parents would not think of their children as lonely and miserable. Later, when the children were no longer homesick and would have resented the time wasted on communication with their families, there was no pressure on them and no additional pain to the parents from the fact that their children no longer wanted any contact with them. Everything went much more smoothly with the "clean break" policy.

Why did I, as a writer, avoid developing a relationship between Ender and his parents?

As a writer, I have learned how very difficult and complicated it is to set characters in a community where they have the full range of human relationships. Every person is a different character in each of his relationships. Our brains have the remarkable ability to sort out our memories, attitudes, even mannerisms, so that we behave differently with each person we have an important relationship with.

We see this all the time; we *do* this ourselves. We have our "telephone voice," our "meeting a stranger" attitude. We have the friends whom we immediately start joking with in a certain way, and the ones with whom our conversations are more analytical. If you're ever away from a close friend from an earlier phase of your life and then meet up with them again after many years, you almost invariably find yourself becoming the person you were back when you were close. It can be quite surprising to realize that the "old you" is still there inside you, waiting for the trigger of that old relationship to wake up that hidden personality.

This is what "characterization" really is, in fiction writing—and, I might add, in acting as well. Too many people think characterization is about finding an interesting backstory for the character, or inventing quirks and eccentricities and mannerisms. Those are actually cheap tricks; it's what you do to make characters memorable without actually having to create them with any depth.

Instead, real characterization is figuring out who they are, what attitude and manner they present, in *each* of their significant relationships. This is hard work!

And that's why most fiction is centered around a character who is a functional adolescent—that is, a person who is disconnected from family and wandering through the world making no lasting relationships beyond the level of bonhomie. Think of Han Solo and Chewbacca, and you get the idea; each one has his mannerisms, and they do not change from person to person. They present the same face to everyone.

Then think of the trio of characters at the heart of Lord of the Rings: Frodo, Sam, and Gollum. Each of them is a different person with each of the others. Frodo speaks to Sam very differently from the way he speaks to Gollum; Gollum treats Sam and Frodo differently; Sam shifts from pert servant with Frodo to hostile overlord with Gollum. Add to this the complexity that Gollum is truly of two minds, so that there is a duality within him that is only occasionally visible to the others, and you end up with an extremely intricate web of relationships.

That's with three people. Now put a character into a family—parents, siblings. Give him a job—boss, co-workers. Then add in some friends—old friends, new friends—and romantic interests, and the job of characterization becomes daunting indeed.

Which is why most writers avoid the whole situation. All relationships are shallow; "characters" are one thing all the time. They feel like cardboard because they are—a picture that is merely turned to face each other person in turn, with no changes.

Now remember that *Ender's Game* was written very early in my career. The short story was my first sale—my first real attempt at real sci-fi storytelling. The novel was among my first ten, and I was still using what we call Romantic storytelling—that adolescent hero, disconnected from others as he moves through the world.

It wasn't until after I wrote *Ender's Game* that I began to work with characterization in complex groups. With *Wyrms*, the novel I wrote between *Ender's Game* and *Speaker for the Dead*, I assembled a group of characters, most of them representatives of different species and therefore easy to characterize using eccentricities that they presented to everyone the same way. But in the relationships between the heroine, Patience, and the humans in her life—her father, the ship's pilot, her mentor, and Will, the man she would fall in love with—I had to show her becoming a different person with each.

Then, with *Speaker for the Dead*, I brought Ender Wiggin, as a thirty-year-old, into a pre-existing family which consisted of a complicated mother, a dead father whose abusiveness had colored all their lives, and multiple siblings who presented different attitudes to each of the others and to Ender himself.

I was a hundred pages into the first draft of the post-*Ender's Game* version of *Speaker* when I showed it to my friend and fellow-writer Gregg Keizer. Gregg's forthright comment was devastating: When Ender met the children of the family, it was boring because he couldn't tell the children apart.

That was my wake-up call. I couldn't separate the children by making them each of a different species, as I had done with the traveling party in *Wyrms*. They were all human, yet had to be clearly different from each other. That was when I learned the principle of finding quick and easy distinguishing markers to differentiate them at first, and then gradually revealing the really complex characters later, as scenes unfold and relationships develop and clarify. It's very hard work, but I think I learned the lesson well and have used it ever since.

It's worth saying that I had actually used complex characterization before, in my novel *Saints*, but there I was basing the characters on historical people, and I had three times the length to work with, so their natures could be revealed by their choices over time. This is simple "Romantic characterization," in which the characters are what they do, but in *Saints* they had time to do so many things, for so many reasons, that complex characterization developed without my really understanding what I was doing. So I didn't acquire complex characterization then as a tool I could then apply to other books.

With *Ender's Game*, the family section was a throwaway—I rushed through that section merely to get Ender to Battle School as quickly but as interestingly as possible. I knew he needed to come from a family; I used a shallow version of my own situation with my own older siblings (I'm a third child), as I conceived them when I was about Ender's age.

To a child that age, siblings are the ones that must be negotiated with; parents are simply a given. Parents are what they are and do what they do; they're like tides, like air, like weather. But siblings are potential rivals and allies. Their relationships shift constantly as they reach different levels of maturity and physical size. Thus I developed Ender's relationships with Peter and Valentine with clarity, even in Ender's absence, while leaving his relationships with his parents as a generic fog. On good days I'd call this a writing strategy; on bad days,

I'd call it laziness, or mere inattention as I rushed forward to the "real" story.

When I wrote those first chapters of *Ender's Game*, I had no plan to use Peter and Valentine or the parents again until the end of the book. But Peter and Valentine, shallow as their characterization was in the first chapter, became so interesting to me that I found a use for them, which became an entire subplot that allowed me to show what was happening on Earth while Ender was in Battle School.

In the process, I developed them as full characters, and began to wake the parents up a little—though they were still filtered through the perceptions of their more-than-slightly arrogant children. It was not until the later Shadow books that I created Ender's parents as real people. In *Ender's Game* they remained only what Peter and Valentine thought they were—easily fooled people who had no idea what was going on.

One thing I was certain of in writing the novel: I was never going to use the parents' point of view. Nor was I even going to use them in the dialogues at the beginnings of the chapters—those spots were reserved for adults in the IF who were talking about Ender Wiggin and/or the war.

So, as a writer, I left the parents passive primarily because the cost of developing them as characters would have been too high, and would not have added anything to the story I had to tell. You can't tell everything; you can't develop everything; and so I essentially set the parents aside and concentrated on Ender Wiggin with his siblings and then with the complicated Battle School community.

I have become a much more skilled and self-aware writer since I created the novel *Ender's Game* back in 1984. If I were writing it for the first time today, I would probably not spend any more *time* on Ender's parents, but I would make them a bit more interesting and complicated, and I would give them a bit more of a role in his inner life at school. Compare the way I treated them with the way I treated Bean's "parent," Sister Carlotta, in *Ender's Shadow*.

But since the novel has done reasonably well without my having spent more time on the parents, I must say what I always say about the deficiencies of my early work: I did the best I knew how to do at the time with the story that I intended to tell.

—*OSC*

Q. How did you feel when Apple completely ripped off your Desk design for the iPad?

A. They're still so far from my vision of the Desk that I can only view the iPad as a step in the right direction.

—OSC

WINNING AND LOSING IN ENDER'S GAME

HILARI BELL

M any years ago, during the Summer Olympic Games, Nike ran a series of ads that made me crazy. I forget most of the narrative, but the tagline was, "There's only one winner," followed by a clear implication that everybody else was just dust on the winner's Nikes. I hated those ads. Everyone who goes to the Olympics is a brilliant athlete to start with. The distance between first and second place, sometimes even first and fourth or fifth or sixth place, is a fraction of a second, a breath, a single missed step. Everyone at the Olympics is a winner, and the difference between them is usually almost nothing. The Nike ads' statement that only the person who happened to finish first mattered, and everyone else was worthless, made me furious.

I imagined a whole series of counter ads, which told the splendid, heroic stories of the people who didn't win— who sometimes didn't even place. Of the distance runner with the injured leg who hobbled into the stadium long after the race was over and the crowd had gone—who knew he hadn't a hope of winning, but he'd come there to *run*, even if only his coach and the janitors sweeping up the trash were there to see him limp across the finish line. Of the Iditarod racer who saw an empty dogsled running by, and lost his place to go looking for his fallen competitor—the woman had a concussion, and might have frozen to death if he hadn't found her.

There are definitions of "winning" that are more subtle than beating an opponent. Simply succeeding, in business or life, can be regarded as winning. So can achieving a high level of skill—as when I said that "everyone at the Olympics is a winner." But most of those definitions come from our softer modern time. In the old definitions, like the Nike ads, to win you have to beat someone else. Even in the bad old days, though, winning wasn't always the ultimate goal.

The phrase *Pyrrhic victory* comes from a battle where General Pyrrhus beat the Romans at such great cost of life and resources that he later lost the war. And there are plenty of modern real-life situations where winning can lose you far more than you gain from it. Arguing with your boss comes to mind. Or your spouse. And have you ever noticed that the people who insist on winning all the time are people no one wants to hang out with?

Ultimately, I ended up writing a pile of novels where winning cost more than losing would have. Or where the hero deliberately chose to lose instead of win because losing gained him more in the end. But I have to say, I have never encountered any book—including my own—in which "winning" is as hollow, as devastating, as worthless, as it is in *Ender's Game.*

The first question you have to ask about winning is: *Who are you trying to beat? Who is your opposition? Who's the enemy?* In the future Earth of *Ender's Game*, the Formic War has reshaped all of human society—and that world-shaking alien threat is still there. But the real enemy in *Ender's Game* is not the formics but Ender's teachers.

From the start, the teachers set out to isolate Ender, first from his family, then from all the friends and allies he makes throughout the book—completely overlooking the fact that Ender's real genius, his real strength, comes from his ability to build alliances. Even as a launchie, he triumphs over Bernard by making friends, first with the outcasts, Dap and Shen, and then with the other boys, starting with Alai. Yes, Ender hacks the Battle School's computer system to start the process. And later, he uses his brilliance to win his armies' games. But the computer and really even the battle games are primarily tools that Ender uses to bring allies onto his side. Allies against whom? The formics, at this point, are so distant from Ender's thoughts that they hardly register. Allies to help him win the games, certainly. But mostly, in the beginning, what Ender is really fighting for is survival against the world the teachers have created.

It always surprises me that the fictional villains who set out to create genius super-soldiers, who they plan to control by brainwashing and torture, never stop to think that sooner or later their super-powered geniuses are bound to realize that their creators are the bad guys. The super-soldier has been bred/mutated/modified to be really, really smart, right? And the evil creator thinks this genius is not going to figure out that the bad guy has been brainwashing him, and ultimately turn the tables on his creator, *why*? Haven't any of them read Shelley? Because, even when, as in *Frankenstein*, the monster is destroyed in the end of the story, he always takes his evil creator down with him. My favorite example of this theme is in the Lois McMaster Bujold novel *Brothers in Arms*, where the evil creator has been brainwashing and torturing the (teenage) super-soldier throughout his young life. In the climax, Evil Creator hands the soldier a gun and tells him he has one last lesson to learn; he must learn to kill his enemy. And the young soldier promptly shoots Evil Creator.

How much more likely does this scenario become if the super-soldier/monster is a genius? *I've designed this monster to be way smarter than me, and I've been tormenting him for years to keep him under my control.* And this seems like a good idea?

Mind you, brainwashing does work. Fictional heroics aside, humans are pack animals—we have a huge, hard-wired drive to fit in with, and earn the approval of, the people around us. Particularly if we're placed under stress, we need the support of other humans, so we do what they want. This is the mechanism that lies at the heart of Stockholm syndrome, where victims bond with their kidnappers. It's also why agents under deep cover for a long time tend to forget which side they're on and, for that matter, why having high expectations for a class of students brings out the best in them. The human desire to conform to a group, to win and keep a place in it, makes us really malleable by the people around us.

The other side of that coin is that, as soon as the brainwashee gets out from under the thumb of his captor and starts being exposed to new people with new expectations, he starts bonding with his new pack—and the brainwashing wears off. However, in *Ender's Game*, this isn't a problem for the teachers because Ender is never able to escape the twisted, encompassing universe his creators have invented.

But Ender really is a genius, and even living in the worldwide lie his teachers have created doesn't stop him from recognizing his true enemy. Being a genius, and a profoundly empathetic one as well, Ender sees through his teachers almost from the start. He understands what they're doing, and why. The teachers really are trying to save the world—they're just willing to make and break children in order to do it.

In Salamander, Ender befriends Petra, to learn from her, and he keeps his old alliance of launchies together, despite the fact that it's "not done." He also watches how Bonzo fails, despite the discipline he imposes, because his soldiers don't have any independence—they're obeyers, not allies. And how, because of that, Bonzo's team loses.

In Rat, Ender befriends the competent Dink. And again, instead of abandoning his old alliances, he keeps them intact, even when past allies become his opponents in the Battle School games. And because of that, they all win, in the softer sense, by becoming better, stronger, more competent, more able.

Dink is the first to introduce the question of who the real enemy is: "These other armies, they aren't the enemy. It's the teachers, they're the enemy. They get us to fight each other, to hate each other. The game is everything. Win win win. It amounts to nothing."

But Ender, who sees his teachers even more clearly than Dink, doesn't agree. He believes the formics are real. That Battle School *is* more than a game—that the threat that drives the teachers is real. Because of that, he's willing "for them to make me into a tool. To save the world." Ender becomes a willing sacrifice—because, like the teachers, he believes the ends justify it.

Then one of the games ends in a physical attack on Ender, real injuries are dealt out—and the teachers let it slide, passing off the other boys' broken bones as an accident. This fight isn't an abstraction, like saving the world. Faced with real blood and real pain, Ender begins to wonder if Dink might be right.

> And then a worse fear that he *was* a killer, only better at it than Peter ever was, and that it was this very trait that pleased the teachers. It's killers they need for the bugger wars.

Ender is also suffering profoundly under the teachers' rule. Too much isolation, too much torment, is how monsters are created. Even as Ender becomes a more perfect killing tool, he hates what the teachers are making of him, and soon begins to hate them as well.

But he does like winning the games. Eventually, with his record of wins unbroken, he becomes almost addicted to the high of winning, of struggling to achieve the victory. He must win every match, no matter what the cost in exhaustion, and in friendship:

> "What's the worst that could happen? You lose one game."
>
> "Yes, that's the worst that could happen. I can't lose *any* games. Because if I lose *any*—"

Ender's constant successes only add to his isolation, making him first a teacher himself, and later a commander. But in order to win the games, Ender is willing to pay that price.

Nike would have loved this kid.

Outside of the games, winning is a different, darker matter. In the real fights Ender gets into, fights that end in blood and pain, he hates the damage he inflicts. Even in the fight that breaks out within the game, which first leads him to doubt his teachers, Ender hates having to hurt anyone. The fight with Bonzo, which comes later, almost destroys him: "I'm sick of the game. No game is worth Bonzo's blood, pinking the water on the bathroom floor. Ice me, send me home, I don't want to play anymore."

There's another aspect of Ender's world where winning, and its price, is thoroughly explored—the computer game, which takes images from Ender's own mind, his own subconscious, and creates a world for him to battle his way through. I frequently find myself calling it "the dream world" because it's so full of Ender's dreams and nightmares. And this is a world in which winning, which Ender loves, and killing, which he hates, are remorselessly linked.

The only way to get past the Giant is to burrow into its eye and kill it—Ender's only choice is between "his own grisly death and an even worse murder. I'm a murderer, even when I play. Peter would be proud of me." Winning this way leaves Ender feeling not triumphant but sickened and ashamed.

Killing the wolf children in the computer world leaves him aching to "go to one of the villages and become one of the little boys working and playing there, with nothing to kill and nothing to kill me, just living there."

In the world of the computer game, winning means killing—and killing holds nothing but pain and shame. When Ender finally kills the serpent, the face he sees in the mirror is Peter's face—he sees, in the most graphic fashion possible, that killing is making him into a monster.

Meanwhile, Valentine and Peter have created their own alliance—an alliance of enemies, who are using each other to win, even though they recognize that the other might turn and destroy him or her at any moment. When Ender starts to burn out in despair, one of his teachers goes to Valentine, to make her write a letter persuading Ender to fight on. But Ender isn't fooled—he recognizes Valentine's letter as yet another tool the teachers are using to shape him into their weapon.

> The one real thing, the one real precious thing was his memory of Valentine, the person who loved him before he ever played a game, who loved him whether there was a bugger war or not, and they had taken her and put her on their side. She was one of them now. He hated them and all their games.

Now, Ender is ready to acknowledge them fully as his
enemy. He wants to quit—but trapped in the world the
teachers have created, even as he recognizes that he's been
trapped, Ender can't quit.

Raised to the command of Dragon, Ender sets up his
whole team as an alliance, right from the start, creating
teams that can act independently while working together
to fulfill their common goal. He even makes an ally of Carn
Carby and other defeated enemies by sharing his tactics
with those who are willing to listen to him, by gaining their
respect. Ender is still profoundly lonely, but at this point,
he has realized that, as a commander, sometimes he'll have
to sacrifice friendship for alliance—to give up being part of
the community to make his army stronger. He maintains his
old personal alliances with Dink and Petra, even when he
defeats them. And finally, in the ultimate act of alliance, he
reveals weakness to Bean, a subordinate—which not only
welds Bean to him, but lets Ender begin to rely on his allies'
strengths, not just his own.

> "They can't break you."
>
> "You'd be surprised." Ender breathed sharply,
> suddenly, as if there were a stab of pain, or he had
> to catch a sudden breath in a wind; Bean looked at
> him and realized that the impossible was happen-
> ing. Far from baiting him, Ender Wiggin was actu-
> ally confiding in him. Not much. But a little. Ender
> was human, and Bean had been allowed to see.
>
> "Maybe you'll be surprised," said Bean.
>
> "There's a limit to how many clever new ideas
> I can come up with every day. Somebody's going

to come up with something to throw at me that I haven't thought of before, and I won't be ready ... I need you to be clever, Bean. I need you to think of solutions to problems we haven't seen yet. I want you to try things no one has ever tried, because they're absolutely stupid."

This is also when Ender first begins to study the formics, to learn not just about them but from them. If your teachers are your enemies, then why not let another enemy teach you?

When Bonzo and some of the other boys plot to kill him, it's Ender's friends and allies, not the teachers, who warn him. But Ender still believes the teachers will prevent him from being killed; if they value him, which their training surely indicates, then at least they must need him alive.

However, when Bonzo and his gang corner Ender in the shower, Dink is the only one who comes to his aid, and it's Dink who gets Ender out after the fight ends. The teachers' failure to show up to save him is Ender's final proof that they're his real enemy. He condemns them for "their stupidity or cruelty or whatever it was that made them let it happen."

Right after this traumatic fight, the teachers thrust Ender's army into the battle game against two other armies. And once he's won, Ender reveals to the teachers that he knows who his enemies really are:

> "I beat you again, sir," he said.
> "Nonsense, Ender," Anderson said softly. "Your battle was with Griffin and Tiger."
> "How stupid do you think I am?"

But even when Ender refuses to play anymore, he still can't escape the trap, for when he goes on strike, they bring in Valentine to persuade him to go on. She tells Ender that he can win by controlling the teachers, as she and Peter are beginning to control their world. Ender could control the teachers—it's his ability to understand people, deep down, that lets him win, and he understands his teachers very well. But to understand someone that well, for Ender, is to love them too. It's that love that prevents him from ever becoming a real monster, like Frankenstein's monster. Like Peter.

Seeing the teachers so clearly, and having been granted access to films of the last invasion, only confirms that they're telling the truth about the formic threat. Ender decides to go on to Command School. He decides for himself to "become exactly the tool you want me to be ... but at least I won't be *fooled* into it. I'll do it because I choose to, not because you tricked me, you sly bastard." Because for Ender, the survival of the human race is more important than whether or not the teachers win. This battle isn't a game.

At Command School, Ender is given access to all available information about the formics, and he begins to know them well enough to love and to destroy them. He's also given a companion, Mazer. A teacher who is Ender's avowed enemy from the very start—the ultimate monster maker.

> "I am your enemy, the first one you've ever had who was smarter than you. There is no teacher but the enemy ... I am your enemy from now on. From now on, I am your teacher."

But as Mazer teaches him more about the formics, Ender questions whether the war is truly necessary—if the humans really have to win.

> "So the whole war is because we can't talk to each other."
> "If the other fellow can't tell you his story, you can never be sure he isn't trying to kill you."
> "What if we just left them alone?"

In other words: *What if they stop trying to win? What if they stop playing altogether?*

But the teachers believe that humanity can't risk doing anything but fight, and to help him do so, Ender is given back his alliances—the army he shaped so well in Battle School. The games begin again. Mazer, the declared enemy, fights against Ender with all he's got—and Ender, thinking he's fighting the worst of his teachers, all the teachers, beats Mazer. Or so he believes.

> Ender didn't understand. It seemed all wrong. They were supposed to be angry... He tried to make sense of this. Had he passed the test after all? It was *his* victory, not theirs, and a hollow one at that, a cheat; why did they act as if he had won with honor?

Mazer and the rest of Ender's teachers are acting that way because they *did* win. Ender learns that, all unknowing, he's been fighting a real war, with real weapons, against a real enemy. And he's won. The formics have been destroyed; the humans have won. The teachers have won.

Ender's victory is devastating, not only to his enemy and the army he didn't know he was wielding, but to him: "I killed them all, didn't I?...All their queens. So I killed all their children. All of everything."

And the teachers even acknowledge exactly what they did: "You had to be a weapon, Ender. Like a gun, like the Little Doctor, functioning perfectly but not knowing what you were aimed at. *We* aimed you. We're responsible."

The teachers told this lie, committed this betrayal, because they knew that if Ender knew the truth, he couldn't, *wouldn't* have done it.

> "If you knew, you couldn't do it. If you were the kind of person who would do it even if you knew, you could never have understood the buggers well enough."

In winning, Ender has lost. The teachers have successfully used his empathy, his ability to build alliances, his ability to see into people and to love them, to destroy their enemy. And in doing so, they have in fact succeeded in making Ender into a monster. A xenocide. They've lied him into becoming Peter.

They made their monster, aimed him like a weapon . . . and won. Unlike in *Frankenstein*, unlike all the books where the super-soldier—whether he dies or not—takes his evil creator down, in *Ender's Game* the bad guys win it all. And those bad guys not only win and survive, they retire, and despite the inconvenience of a court trial—in which they get acquitted—they live happily ever after.

You could claim that when Peter, who truly is a monster, becomes the ruler of the world, the bad guys are getting what they deserve. But Peter has learned to conceal his sadistic streak, to become a statesman. And though I don't believe for a minute that the world wouldn't be better off with someone sane ruling it, the bad guys don't know that.

After this last battle, it's Ender's allies, Petra, Alai, Dink, and Bean, who rouse Ender from his depression and bring him back to life. It's Valentine, fleeing her alliance with Peter, who takes Ender to the formics' empty world. In that world, among the bones of the Giant who was his first deliberate kill, Ender finds a message that the formic queen he killed has left for him.

He learns the devastating truth that his victory was even more hollow than he'd believed, that once they'd realized that individual humans were sentient, the formics had no intention of killing them. But the message from the queen also offers Ender a chance to reverse his xenocide, to bring back the people he destroyed.

> "I'll carry you," said Ender. "I'll go from world to world until I find a time and a place where you can come awake in safety. And I'll tell your story to my people, so that perhaps in time they can forgive you, too. The way that you've forgiven me."

Forgiveness, the chance for redemption, hope, and peace are finally given to the monster—but not by the *winners*. These gifts don't come from the people who shaped him and used him, whose world he saved. The gifts that let

Ender go forward healed and at peace come from the *losers*. The people he beat. The people he destroyed.

In Ender's game, winning is the province of the enemy and brings only pain. True strength comes not from being the best—which Ender is—but from alliance, teamwork, friendship…and the losers. It's a very stark world. But it's one hell of an answer to those Nike commercials.

Hilari Bell writes SF and fantasy for kids and teens, including the Farsala Trilogy, the Knight & Rogue series, and the Raven Duet. Her favorite hobby is "decadent" camping, because that's the only time she gets to do enough reading—though when it comes to reading, there's no such thing as enough. Her website is www.hilaribell.com.

Q. If you could go back and re-write *Ender's Game*, what would you change? Is there something that has always bothered you, something you wrote that you now think is silly, or something you wish you would have included?

A. You can see which things I would change by noticing what I *have* changed in *Ender's Shadow* and *Ender in Exile*, and what I have re-explained in *First Meetings* and other Ender-related stories. *Ender's Game* was written with only one sequel in mind—*Speaker for the Dead*. *Ender's Game* represented the best I could do at the time with the story I was telling, but it would be depressing indeed if I had not learned a great deal more about writing and everything else in the years since then.

But it is also true that, while I have written many books that I regard as better—truer, deeper, more important, more technically expert, and more artistically pleasing—I have written no novel that has resonated with the public to the degree that *Ender's Game* has.

There *is* a novel that I completely re-wrote after learning much more about my craft, and about everything else. My first novel, *Hot Sleep*, was structurally a mess. A few years later, after I had learned a lot about novel writing, I rewrote it completely as *The Worthing Chronicle*, which now forms the major part of the book *The Worthing Saga*. But *The Worthing Chronicle* did not resonate with the audience the way *Hot Sleep* did; despite all the improvements (and there were many!) between the versions, I also apparently lost something. Freshness, perhaps; the vigor of first-telling; the very naivete that was both flaw and irreplaceable virtue.

So it is safe to say that, were I writing *Ender's Game* today, it would be very different in the manner of the telling, but I do not have any reason to believe that it would be better, or more effective as storytelling.

I am lucky, as a writer, to have one book that resonates with the public as *Ender's Game* does. At the same time, I must point out that at some time *every* book of mine has been singled out by one or more readers as their absolute favorite, as my "best." All these stories have a reason to exist; they all tell some kind of truth about human life as best I understand it; and if some have larger audiences than others, that is only to be expected.

But I have no intention of doing a complete overhaul of *Ender's Game*. I am preparing an edition that reconciles a few contradictions between *Ender's*

Game and the later-written books, just as Tolkien revised *The Hobbit* slightly to bring the ringlore of that book into line with what was required by the later Lord of the Rings. But these are changes of detail, not serious revisions. I am quite content with *Ender's Game* as it stands.

—*OSC*

PARALLAX REGAINED

Two Views of *Ender's Game*

DAVID LUBAR AND
ALISON S. MYERS

Introduction #1: On the Origin of Thesis

My daughter and I have much in common. We both would rather lose a pint of blood than an argument. We both were raised by book-loving parents (heh, heh). And we both seem to have a knack for finding creative solutions to problems—especially those problems that would go away if left alone.

When I was asked to write an essay about *Ender's Game*, it dawned on me that, despite our commonalities and our 50 percent identical DNA, my daughter and I approach the book from a variety of opposed perspectives. As a writer whose books are often assigned to students for required reading, I'm on the supply side of publishing and education. As a teacher who has taught science fiction and AP English, my daughter is on the demand side. I'm male, she's

female. I'm her parent, she's my (grown) child. I grew up
in a world without the internet; she can text with her eyes
closed. My speculative preference as a young adult was for
science fiction, hers was for fantasy. Even where there are
commonalities, we diverge. Though we both studied philosophy, having fallen in love with it at the first sip, my focus was logic and computability, hers was ethics, identity,
and responsibility.

I can think of no approach to this essay that is more
exciting, and potentially more revealing, than to hold a discussion with her about our perceptions of and reactions to
Ender's Game. Our conversation will definitely be a discussion, not an argument. At the moment, I don't have any
pints of blood to spare. And I hate to lose.

In the interest of starting off in a balanced fashion, I'll
now pass the pen over to her for the second introduction.

Introduction #2: Speaker for the Daughter

I grew up trying to foster everything that was the opposite
of my parents: if they suggested a book, I refused to read it.
If something was forbidden, it became all the more tempt-
ing. This benefited both of us: when I was told to go to bed,
I thought that staying up to read under my covers with a
flashlight was a great and noble act of rebellion (and it probably was part of my parents' plan the whole time).

I don't remember my dad suggesting I read *Ender's
Game* when I was younger for this very reason: he'd never
suggest such a sacred text to someone who'd reject it only
because it was recommended by a parent. And although I

discovered its brilliance only later, as an adult, it was as an adult who would be telling kids to read the book after being given *Ender's Game* as one novel in the curriculum for a science fiction course I was teaching.

My dad and I are coming from similar and dissimilar places, and a dialogue seems a natural way to approach these opposing viewpoints: much like Graff and Anderson's discussions at the beginning of each chapter, a philosophical dialogue is a candid look at all of these viewpoints. Both of us are stubborn enough to refuse to be the interlocutor, so I'll default to the older and wiser of the two of us to begin.

D: I'm not sure when I read *Ender's Game* for the first time. I re-read it in 1998 at the suggestion of my editor at Starscape (a Tor imprint that had just released a new edition of the book for younger readers). He felt the Graff sections would give me some ideas about how to reveal more of the world in the novel I was working on because my novel was written from the first-person viewpoint of a single character. I was definitely inspired by this technique.

A: And I read it for the first time as a teacher. To teach about a six-year-old's coming of age to a class of seniors in the spring is like handing them the best skydiving manual an hour before they're going to be pushed out of the plane.

These kids are about to experience the ultimate monitor-removal: leaving school. And just as Ender worries about becoming like Peter now that his monitor is gone, students graduating from high school are faced with radical freedom as well as with what could be debilitating responsibility to fulfill the expectations that have been set for them, and their new ontological status as "graduates." The depth and extremity of Ender's isolation from everything safe—his parents, his sister, his home, and even his planet—parallels the approaching graduation. Ender still has the choice of whether to go to Battle School. My students have a choice in their future, but it's likewise unknown and scary. Students are also leaving what's comfortable and familiar. By leaving home, they're approaching complete responsibility for all of the decisions they'll make in their lives.

D: Though they may be leaving one home, part of growing up is finding your own home (even if you have to take a slight detour and save humanity from extermination before you get a chance to start apartment hunting). But to the parent, the child who moves out will always have two homes (unless the homes are separated by interplanetary distances).

A: And this is part of the "master of two worlds" that my students become once they graduate: when they leave for college, they have a college "home" and a hometown "home"—it's reconciling the two, much like reconciling being a soldier and a friend (like Ender), that's difficult. Ender has to find a way to fulfill the expectations set for him by his soldiers as

well as his teachers. He has an ultimate mission—
saving humanity—and several local missions—peer
acceptance, platoon success, and self-preservation—
at the same time.

What one could read as Ender's goal, to be un-
forgettable, is cemented early in the novel. "They
won't forget me," he says, after he beats the older
boys at the holographic game. This is something that
seniors can all relate to: part of embarking on adulthood is thinking about what you're leaving at your
high school. Students want to leave a mark on their
school—whether they want to write the best paper
you'll ever read or be the worst-behaved kid you've
ever seen.

D: Those goals don't end with graduation. Some writers write to be immortal, or at least, like your students, to make a mark. That creates a "be careful
what you wish for" scenario. Most successful writers
see a dynamic change in the way they are treated
by their peers after they break in. (Writers are just
as cliquish as students. We've merely swapped the
cafeteria for conventions, pubs, listservs, and other
gathering spots.) It's okay to be successful but not
too successful. I think the scene in chapter eleven
where the commanders react to Ender's success is a
perfect metaphor for the way I suspect some writers
responded to Scott after the rise of *Ender's Game*. Revealing more of my dark side than is wise, I'll admit

it is easier for me to like and applaud books that broke out before I broke in.

A: I often hear kids telling each other to be mindful of the pitfalls of success, especially envy—particularly when it comes to bullying. Unless they know they won't be ridiculed for outstanding success, they want to stay safely in the middle, for fear of those who pick out and try to destroy the eccentric or the talented outliers.

D: Ironically, it's often the outlier who becomes the writer—assuming he survives the bullying.

A: Growing up is painful.

D: As is observing that growth.

A: But it's part of the "human condition" that I talk about so much in my classes, and the fear of the unknown, of not knowing "the plan." In Ender's case, and unbeknownst to him, the plan actually exists.

Graff says, "He can never come to believe that anybody will ever help him out, ever. If he once thinks there's an easy way out, he's wrecked." Throughout the years that I've been teaching, I've always had at the foundation of my pedagogy the idea that teaching is the gradual transfer of responsibility from myself to my students. Ideally, they all leave me completely comfortable in their autonomy, and ready to enter the "real world"—which is a phrase with intriguing

implications in *Ender's Game*. There's an interesting relationship between practice and reality, where
when you're in "practice," there's still a degree of reality to it, but in reality—haha –all practice is reality.
When we think we're preparing for the next stage,
we're still in a reality.

D: And in reality, we all strive to know the plan—
which brings us to one of the many masterful elements of this book. Ender is facing the unknown.
But we aren't. One reason the book absorbs the
reader is that *we know the plan*. Graff says what he is
going to do to Ender. We're now being prodded by
a two-pronged suspense fork. We not only wonder
what exactly will happen—how Graff will carry out
that plan—we also wonder how much Ender will
figure out. For Ender, the story is a mystery. For the
reader, it is a suspense novel. Though we are both
led blindfolded to the final twist. (The reader has a
much easier journey than Ender.)

The chapter openings are a brilliant way to show
things that Ender doesn't know because most of the
book is written from Ender's third-person limited
viewpoint. I suspect that writers are much more
aware of viewpoint shifts than most readers. For
those who want to study such things, take note of
the places where we see a scene from Valentine's or
Bean's viewpoint, and take special note of the way
Ender's first-person thoughts are presented without
the traditional use of italics.

A: And stylistically, this makes his thoughts homogeneous with the narration.

D: The very first use of first person for Ender's thoughts takes place in Ender's opening scene, and is introduced not with "he thought" or with italics but by smoothly transitioning from an action ("tried to imagine") to the thought that arose from the action: "Ender tried to imagine the little device missing from the back of his neck. I'll roll over on my back and it won't be pressing there."

A: This sets the tone for the reader for the rest of the novel; it leads the reader to understand that she *will* be privy to Ender's thoughts. Ender and the reader are intimate from the beginning—she can trust Ender to tell her the truth and the way that things really are.

D: Speaking of trust and intimacy, I find it fascinating that we get the shift to first person for Ender, Valentine, and even Bean, but not for Peter. Peter, alone, remains shadowy, never fully revealed by the tools of viewpoint. The problem is, writers can do all these brilliant things, and then they wait for someone to notice them. Writing is one of the most difficult art forms for those who crave a response. (I plead guilty to this weakness. Validation is my drug of choice.) If I paint or draw, I can get immediate feedback or at least validation in the form of a gasp of delight when I unveil the canvas. If I compose, you merely have to sit back and listen while my music plays. No real effort is required. But if I want you to respond to a novel, I need patience on my part and effort on yours.

A. And this is exactly what teaching is like—the time and patience that go into guiding a student to becoming whoever she will be doesn't have immediate rewards (aside from the occasional parent-mandated thank-you note at the end of the year).

D: Happily, most of your work stays in print for many decades. And if you teach for long enough, you'll even get to work on sequels.

A: And I frequently teach different editions. Sometimes I've taught several kids from the same family.

D: Of course, like most analogies, this one offers interesting contrasts. A book reaches many people for a brief period (though the memory can last a lifetime). A teacher reaches fewer people but for a prolonged interaction.

A: As a teacher, you may change a student's life (for better or worse!), but part of the job is being okay with the idea that you might never know the impact you have. I can see how writers and teachers are both creators, but with a teacher, so much depends on the student. Two autonomous agents are working toward (again, hopefully) the same goal—learning, growth, and development. Creating a future.

D: And just as teachers sometimes receive amazing letters from former students, either at graduation time or many years later, most writers can tell wonderful stories of getting "you changed my life" letters, like the one Scott shared in the introduction to the definitive edition of *Ender's Game*.

On the other hand, writing a popular book means you are forced to become, to some degree, a public person. The bigger the book, the more the world sees you as their own. Given that most writers tend to be introverts, this can be a painful transition. In many cases, the successful writer is asked to become a teacher. As in all things, some of us are better at it, and more comfortable with it, than others.

Even if they never enter a classroom, writers are indirect teachers, both through the texts they create and the actions of their characters. For any writer who pays attention to what he reads, *Ender's Game* is a classroom on viewpoint, plotting, pacing, and character development.

A: Ender himself is a better teacher than I could ever hope to be, both to his Battle School troops and to my students—the lessons that he learns are everything that I hope my students take away from high school. I'm lucky to be able to lead my students to Ender, for them to gain these lessons through his experiences.

D: Three responses, if I may.

First, like Ender, you underestimate yourself.

Second, only fictional characters can achieve such a high success rate with their plans. Writers have the pleasure of creating super-human humans. We also have the luxury of second chances. Our characters can succeed, even where we have failed. (I'm not saying Scott flunked out of Battle School or had his monitor yanked after only one week. I'm speaking of writers and life in general.)

Third, the fact that you tied graduation to monitor removal shows you have the kind of creative mind we desperately need in our classrooms. (When I think about graduation and science fiction, the line that comes to mind is, "Danger, Mrs. Robinson!" This helps explain why I don't belong in the classroom.) I can't speak for Scott, but I love it when readers find depth and meaning of this sort in my work, whether or not I put it there, and I suspect most writers feel this way. I try to weave connections into my work at all levels, but readers constantly ask, "Was this intentional?" about things I never intended or even noticed. Making observations and connections, as you did when you linked monitor removal to graduation, is a wonderful activity that enhances the pleasure of reading. I trust you shared some of these observations with your students, and they shared their own observations with you.

A. Definitely. My students have a field day with the names that Scott used—Ender (the one to *end* the war) is a gateway to a discussion like this, but they make the connection that Valentine is the one who loves her brother the most. Peter is the oldest, and many of my students have made a connection to St. Peter (as the foundation and rock of a faith).

Especially on a second pass. *Ender's Game* has so many levels of complexity that, upon a second (or third or twentieth) pass, it gains meaning. On every return to the novel, you bring added experience from your life. This is one of the best parts of revisiting a novel, especially when a marked change has taken place (childhood to adulthood, for example) in the interim, and particularly of revisiting a novel like *Ender's Game*, which has a versatility of compassion for its characters: as an adult and educator, I can feel for both Ender and Graff as teachers in their own respect, but I know that if I read this as a kid, I'd immediately connect to Valentine struggling with the relationship she has with her parents and her brothers.

D: Reading this as a parent, I connected from the other direction. When Valentine realizes her father admires Demosthenes, I felt the power of the scene from the father's perspective, not Valentine's. He appeared to be unaware of major aspects of her life. Though it also reminded me of all the things I hid from my parents.

A: And the things I've hidden from mine. Not that I've ever done that.

D: And not that I've ever secretly known some of those things you've never done. But we'll talk about that later, in private.

A: The concept of parents as autonomous agents reminds me of the realization that my parents are individuals themselves, and don't just exist as extensions of my own life and experiences. Parenthood is an aspect of their lives, not the entirety of it.

D: I'm pleased to have been granted an independent existence by she who I helped bring into existence. This makes me feel like a Borges character or part of an Escher engraving—but in a good way. Getting back to the idea of reader identification (and comfortably away from further discussion of our youthful misadventures)—readers may identify with different secondary characters at different ages, but readers also generally begin a book with a biased view of the main character. Readers assume characters share everything with them, and then are slowly disabused of the connections as they encounter conflicting evidence. Every time I pick up a book, the main character is an adult male of my size, weight, and beliefs. As I read, the attributes I imposed are sliced off like the limbs of the Black Knight in *Monty Python and the Holy Grail*. In *Ender's Game*, as in most well-crafted novels, the reader learns the key differences within the first few pages. It would be jarring, and perhaps even disastrous, to get to page fifty before learning Ender's age.

A: Aside from the age of the reader, one of the most marked differences between readerships is gender. It's common to see my female students read a novel written from a male perspective, but it's less common to see a male student reading a novel that's written from a female perspective.

Ender is of course male, giving male students something in common with him. But Scott also has two incredibly well-crafted and dynamic female characters—Petra and Val. Their strength is important because they don't merely serve supporting roles. They are guides for Ender. Valentine is Ender's Beatrice: Ender's taken this impossible quest with Valentine in mind, unable to envision a world where she's torn apart by formics. And Petra is Ender's Virgil: her guidance, support, and camaraderie give him the confidence to become the leader he needs to be.

D: Writers deal with a certain body of conventional wisdom, including the idea that a girl will read a boy book but a boy won't read a girl book, and that young readers prefer to read about someone two or three years older. Whenever I hear the latter belief mentioned, I point to Ender as a counter example. I suspect, if Valentine got her own novel, she'd be a good counter example for the former belief. I'm glad your students, both male and female, were able to identify with Ender in various and meaningful ways. And I'm pleased you're teaching a novel that taught me so much. However, I can't help wondering about one potential issue for anyone who teaches the book. In the introduction to the definitive edition, Scott mentions that he deliberately avoided "all the little literary games and gimmicks that make 'fine' writing so impenetrable to the general audience." As someone teaching literature not to a general audience but to high school students at the highest levels, does the clarity of the text create any problems in the classroom?

A: I don't think it does—it just opens up an opportunity for students to see the text through different lenses. A text whose literal meaning is clear is more effective on a figurative level. I always teach science fiction with the idea that the genre has allegory at its core. The *science* aspect of science fiction, as well as the fantasy aspect, allows the enjoyer (I always tell my students to avoid writing about "the reader" when they should focus solely on the literature) to understand philosophical and, particularly, ethical issues. A discussion about true happiness is easier to understand if man can widely and readily attain complete physical complacency without repercussions (like the use of soma in *Brave New World*); a dialogue about racism can be easier to explore if you're talking about aliens versus humans.

THREE RIVERS PUBLIC LIBRARY
25207 W. CHANNON DRIVE
P.O. BOX 300
CHANNAHON, IL 60410-0300

Many of the ethical dilemmas brought up in science fiction are timeless, but science fiction's frequent use of emergent technology allows these timeless issues to be tethered to both the science and technology present in the news and the science and technology present in science fiction: video games and the internet have changed the way that we can express and understand the human condition.

D: As someone who was around when the internet was evolving, I can appreciate the ways in which the book came close. The idea of gaining a following is right on target, as is the idea of concealed identities. As for the bloggers influencing or shaping public opinion, that is dead on.

A: The anonymity of the internet became a source of power for Peter and Valentine. Online, the enemy doesn't know if you're a teenage mean girl or a middle-aged socialist. The power that comes with concealing one's identity can allow one to be not just effective, as Peter and Valentine are, but cruel in a way that's safe for the bully.

D: Or the online book reviewer with a grudge.

A: Ender wants to use this kind of anonymity for good, rather than ill, when he identifies himself as "God." We can still, however, see a dichotomy of good and evil in the range of all of the characters' ethical options, and Ender's place in the middle. This power through anonymity is the beginning of Ender's extreme burden of responsibility and his eventual despair: he's constrained by his morals, yet his mind enables him to comprehend and rationalize man's capacity for both good and evil when given any amount of power.

D: Even in the fantasy game, where no real blood is shed, Ender struggles with the morality of his decisions. Though what really caught my interest, as a writer, is that the fantasy game is a volitional dream. The player/dreamer can take conscious actions and has free will, but the results of his actions and the experiences he encounters fall into the realm of fantasy. Every writer writes dream sequences, and most of us would be better off if we then deleted them. (I know from my own failures that it is very easy to let this sort of scene get out of control or become as self-indulgent as bad poetry or unschooled abstract art.) Although Ender does have some brief traditional dreams and nightmares, especially toward the end of the novel, the game allows him to spend an extended time in a world that reflects his deepest thoughts—without it feeling contrived or arbitrary.

A: And in games, you can always get "multiple lives." Second chances exist in video games. It's safe to fail, and it encourages learning. We connect to games, and even project ourselves (in true *Avatar* fashion) onto the pixels that we control. If Link failed to save

Zelda, I failed to save Zelda. If Link died, I died. But we were both reborn. Scott writes the following about Ender's first experiences playing the game: "He had lots of deaths, but that was OK, games were like that, you died a lot until you got the hang of it." Dying is a necessary part of the game and of the learning experience, but this (putting aside all arguments for reincarnation) is impossible for us—to have the opportunity of trial and absolute error, resulting in death, without harming one's self, instead of one's avatar, makes learning available where it otherwise might be impossible.

D: Games allow us to practice making decisions and solving problems without penalty, just as fiction allows us to learn to cope with and process a variety of emotions and situations in a safe environment. I'm not preparing to fight formics, but I have on occasion found myself in micro-versions of some of Ender's dilemmas where I had to rely on my mind to find a way to defeat a physically superior force or avoid an unpleasant task.

A: Video games are more than choose-your-own adventure books; they take away the need for imagination but replace it with a greater (though still finite) amount of free will. A lot of games provide the player with morally ambiguous situations—the heroic Link in *Legend of Zelda* can also throw and slash at chickens in the town, and the protagonist in *Infamous* can choose a good or evil path. The player can choose to be the hero or the villain, making it possible to save humanity or safely play the bad guy.

D: Ender, through the qualities endowed in him by his creator, is more than a hero. Though portrayed as human, he is almost a super-hero. He cannot lose any game or battle. His powers of reasoning allow him to be one step ahead, not just in formal games, but in the larger game of life. This is one of the reasons he is so appealing to the reader. When we read Stephen Gould's *Jumper*, we imagine ourselves with the power of teleportation. When we watch *Spider-Man*, we picture our own silky smooth flight among the skyscrapers. And when we spend time with Ender, we see ourselves triumphing against all challenges.

A: Many of us have experienced the luck of winning when we didn't think we could, but Ender never loses; he always wins. And this could partly be explained by Ender's expectations about his own reactions and the control he exhibits over his emotions. Even when mad, Ender is a "cool" mad, not a "hot" mad, which is ultimately destructive. Using even the most destructive emotion, anger, to propel him forward prioritizes rationality and deliberation in his thought and actions. We all want to know we'll win all of the time, but we don't. Rooting for Ender, and feeling him win and succeed, even when he loses a lot in his sacrifice for it, provides the catharsis that solidifies Ender's place in the pantheon of literary heroes.

D: Perfection is also a powerful dramatic hook. The fact that Ender has never failed yet doesn't guarantee that he will win his final battle. No promise is made to the reader. The fact that we learn of his final victory at the same time that he does bonds us more closely to him by way of both celebration and relief. The wire-walker has reached the platform. Somehow, Ender has survived everything Graff and Mazer have thrown at him. Not only has he survived—he's triumphed, vindicating Graff's cold-blooded methods. As a parent, when I think of Graff's approach I am reminded of my constant battle to allow my child total freedom vs. my instinct to do everything for her and to protect her from all possible harm.

A: And as a child (who has experience as a teacher but not as a parent), I always took comfort in the safety net, even when I was running from it. But Ender is different—for Ender to become the person that the world *needs* him to be, he has to cultivate complete self-reliance. This also brings up the idea of the "easy way out"—sometimes there is none. Sometimes we need to claw through the Giant's eye to survive.

D: This holds true for both characters and their creators. The writers who take the easy way out are not the ones who get published. Or, at least, are not the ones who publish books that endure. If the path is one every reader can immediately see, why bother taking the trip? I suspect it wasn't easy for Scott to kill off characters, even if Ender's victims were unlikeable bullies, or kill off an entire species.

A: Kill your darlings?

D: I can think of no greater proof of good parenting on my part than the fact I taught you that phrase of Faulkner's, and no greater proof of good daughtering (to coin a phrase) than that you remembered it, and knew not only when to pull it from the quiver but how to sharpen the tip with multiple meanings.

A: Archery skill is genetic.

D: Beyond those slain characters, there are many other ways in which Scott doesn't take the easiest way out. The largest of all is in his choice of hero. This is another reason the book is a classic. The easy way to generate empathy is to create a character cut of the same cloth as the reader. It's difficult to get a reader to empathize with a character who is totally unlike the reader in most ways. Nobody who reads *Ender's Game* is six years old, an unwanted third child, and a staggering genius. But we all feel his pain.

A: I think it's Ender's isolation that we can all feel. Many of us are told that we are unique and special and wonderful, but with that comes the isolating aspect of being so unique and special and wonderful. In a way, it's the commonality in our individuality that makes the connection to Ender so instantaneous.

D: Speaking of unique and special and wonderful, daughter dearest, given that you gave me the first word, I'll give you the last.

A: And the last word is almost as good as a parachute.

David Lubar has written thirty books for young readers, including Beware the Ninja Weenies and Other Warped and Creepy Tales *(the seventh book in a series of story collections that have sold more than two million copies), and* Hidden Talents. *His novels are on reading lists across the country, saving countless students from a close encounter with* Madame Bovary. *He has also designed and programmed many video games, but he'd much rather spend his time writing books and trying to gain influence on the internet. In his spare time, he takes naps on the couch. He lives in Nazareth, Pennsylvania, with his wife and various felines. His daughter speaks for herself.*

Alison S. Myers née Lubar teaches high school English and has also saved countless students from a close encounter with Madame Bovary. *She lives with her husband, Mark, and her crazy little shiba, Kira. She* recently developed a Philosophy and Literature class, and is hoping to avoid all offerings of hemlock. Alison also has less to say about herself than her father.

Q. How long was the Battle School open before Ender started? And was it always for children that young?

Did the military always recruit children into Battle School, or did they recruit any genius?

A. Battle School was conceived of as a school *for* children, precisely because they were young enough to be trained out of the gravity-centered mindset of the Earthborn. The school would shape their lives toward war in space from earliest childhood in order to maximize their readiness as adults. But it was not the plan to use them, as children, in combat leadership roles. It was only the calendar that eventually forced that, since by the time the fleets arrived at the formic worlds there was no time for the children who were most skilled to grow up!

Even the first class of Battle School students believed that they might grow up to be the overall commander in the final battles, though of course they had no idea that the battle would not be fought in their solar system. But they expected to take such a position as adults, perhaps after years of experience in fleet maneuvers in real ships.

As the inevitable and unpostponable final battles approached—as the human war fleets prepared to reach their destinations within days of each other—the time for training kept compressing. Since they had not yet found that better-than-Mazer commander when the fleet was ten years out, they knew that the commander, if they found him, would be ridiculously young, and Mazer prepared for command.

Then they found Ender and, a little later, Bean. They knew when Ender came to Battle School that he would have to be made ready by the age of twelve. Thus when they watched him through his monitor, they knew that they only had seven years left. That's why they accelerated his training so radically. Having Bean as possible backup gave them a bit more security, but their ultimate backup was always Mazer Rackham himself.

However, the Battle School experience had gone on long enough for the teachers to see that having children in command would *not* necessarily be a bad thing, as long as they could be shielded from the knowledge of what they were doing. That is because they had long since learned that, like mathematicians, soldiers slow down as they age. Nobody would follow a twelve-year old into battle under ordinary circumstances, yet the twelve-year-old is far quicker of reflex and thought than the same person would be at thirty-two.

Rackham himself could see how much sharper these kids were than he was. It's the experience adults have when children start beating them at videogames. There is a greater depth of knowledge and experience in adults, however, and *that's* what the teachers in Battle School were trying to duplicate in Ender's training. They had to put him in situations that no child would normally be placed in during Battle School, in order to give him a fund of experience that would rival Mazer's own, and make him ready to take command when he was barely twelve years old, for, ready or not, that was when the battle fleets would reach their targets.

So, with the use of children forced upon them, they made a virtue of necessity and then set about framing the situation so that adults *would* follow children into battle and the children *could* command without knowing they were doing so. But by no means was this the original plan when Battle School was founded.

—*OSC*

MIRROR, MIRROR

ALETHEA KONTIS

So you're attending Battle School with Ender and Bean. You've signed your name into the desk (and probably hacked into the teacher accounts) and now it's time for more frivolous pursuits, so you log on to the game. You've passed the Giant's Drink, you've survived Fairyland, and you're standing at the End of the World, looking into the mirror. Who do you see? Ender? Bean? Peter? Valentine?

Mirrors are some of the most powerful objects in literature, and in fairy stories old and new in particular. Mirrors can be used for locating one's enemy (Snow White) or defeating them (Medusa). They are handy when a fictional character needs to travel to another universe (*Through the Looking Glass*), reveal one's heart's desire (Harry Potter), or get insight into one's true inner self (*The Neverending Story*).

Orson Scott Card favored this last one in his famous futuristic fairy tale, *Ender's Game*, but it is not only Ender who gets the chance to have his soul (or his perception of it) reflected back from the mirror's depths. As the mirror at the End of the Universe shows the game player his inner demons, so too does *Ender's Game* itself act as a magic mirror, revealing facets of the Enderverse characters inside each of us.

For we are all characters in the tales of our own lives, are we not? We begin in life as the characters of a story begin: unblemished, untried, and unknowing. We make choices— and mistakes—and we learn from them. And when we are lucky enough to discover characters in literature who are like ourselves, we can look at the choices and mistakes *they* make and learn from those, too. This was the origin of many a fairy story: to warn us of our follies and the dangers of life through hyperbolic example.

As spectacular as Peter, Valentine, Ender, and Bean are, with their mental abilities and special talents, at the core of each of them is a human child with a human heart…just like us. They are identifiable and sympathetic and *personal*. And the extremes to which these characters are pushed, and to which they push themselves, force the reader to question his or her own stamina, willingness, and drive.

Ender

"The most noble title that any child can have is Third."
—Demosthenes

Ender Wiggin is, unsurprisingly, the Hero of the piece.

From the Brothers Grimm to Joseph Campbell, the fairy-tale hero is the quintessential main character. The stakes are high and the odds are against him, but he's resourceful (and stubborn) enough to make it through each challenge, all the way to the end. Sometimes he is the Chosen One, with a destiny he must fulfill. Sometimes he is Jack, the everyman who sets out to find his fortune, usually because his home life is no longer welcoming and he has no choice. In either case, he must conquer the giant, defeat the enemy, and find peace in this world...or some other sort of happy ending. With no guide (and often no parents), he must master his fears and best his foes through his own efforts.

Ender is special—a Third. He carries the weight of the whole world's hope on his shoulders even before his birth. There is a task that only he can perform, and he must leave behind his home and everything he knew to do it. But he is also just an ordinary boy, thrust into extraordinary circumstances, and forced to do the best he can.

Ender is the face we all see in the mirror at one time or another. We have all felt the burden of expectation, whether our own or someone else's. This is particularly true of gifted children. In Ender's world, gifted children are given monitors and sent to Battle School. They are expected to save Earth from the formics. In our world, gifted children are singled out by simply being labeled *gifted* and subsequently burdened with all the baggage that comes with it: the expectation that they will always do a perfect job, without ever screwing up, and that the solutions to problems will come to them easily, every time.

Ender did not choose his abilities. He did not choose to bear the burden of so many hopes and dreams. But that doesn't absolve him of the responsibility to choose what he does with those abilities and those expectations. What Ender does with the hand he is dealt is up to him.

We all sometimes find ourselves stuck in the middle of difficult choices, forced to select the lesser of two evils. We make important choices every day that change the course of our lives, sometimes taking us down dark and dangerous paths with no turning back. Our fate, like Ender's, is in our own hands. We have to learn the rules and play the game so we know how to beat it. It's up to us to populate the long-retired army colors, climb to the top of the leaderboards, and fight our way through to the End of the World.

Bean

> *"I can be the best man you've got, but don't play games with me."*
>
> —BEAN

Bean is the Trickster of the Enderverse.

The Trickster is the hero of his fairy tales, but he is not an obvious hero due to some handicap: his size, his age, his social status, or his financial situation. The Trickster is an outsider whose thoughts and motivations may not be readily clear to the average person. He is a catalyst for change. He may not have brute strength, but he is smarter and quicker and more resourceful than those he must face. Often, he is not fully human. He is the Clever Tailor, who frightens giants by stitching misleading information onto his belt. He is the wise fox who can turn a silly boy into a Count. He is

Tom Thumb, a tiny man born from a wish, who never lets his own stature dictate the size of his adventures.

Ender is incredibly intelligent, but at his core, he is still a very human child. Bean is über-human by design, Frankenstein's monster, an odd duck from his creation, long before he ever got to outer space. Bean is intense and internal. He's the quiet one who sits back and completely thinks out the situation and the people in the situation and the possible outcomes of the situation before he ever says a word… if he even decides to speak. Everything he does has a reason or angle behind it. Emotions confuse him. He teaches himself to respond emotionally when it is expected in a social situation, not when he's actually feeling anything. If he feels anything at all.

And yet, the feelings of being smarter or better or more special, of being different, of being apart from others, are feelings that are all too human. They're quirks shared by any outcast misfit on the fringes of the social order. They are the qualities of the physically handicapped who still maintain every bit of their mental faculties. They are also the main characteristics of autism spectrum disorders (ASDs) like Asperger's, which is frequently linked with creative genius (luminaries such as Isaac Newton, Albert Einstein, Mozart, and even fairy-tale scribe Hans Christian Andersen showed signs of a variety of ASDs).

Bean as Trickster is representative of our shortcomings— be those physical, environmental, or developmental—and of our ability to overcome those obstacles using our wit, resourcefulness, and ability to adapt. Through Bean's story we see that, even if we are at the fringes of society, we too have the ability not just to survive but thrive when faced with such adversity, so long as we keep our wits about us.

Valentine

"You're his monitor now. You better watch him night and day. You better be there."

—Peter

Valentine is in many ways the fairy-tale Princess of *Ender's Game*; she is—as implied by her name—the heart of both *Ender's Game* and Ender himself.

It's one thing for a pure-hearted peasant girl to become a princess by catching a prince's eye (from, say, the top of a tower) or by performing some sort of task (like spinning straw into gold), but kind and gentle princesses in fairy tales who are born to the role seem to have a far more unfortunate lot in life. In most stories, this princess's power—her position, her self-esteem, her rights as a woman—is taken away from her. Briar Rose is cursed before she is old enough to walk or talk, the Goose Girl is forced to switch places with her scheming maid, and Snow White is sent off to be killed by a huntsman. Sometimes the princess gets her power back and finds justice and a happy ending. Sometimes she doesn't.

How easy it is to see Valentine in these roles. Kind and gentle Valentine is always loving but always having her power usurped and stolen away from her. Her generous nature is swept up in Peter's political machinations, his dominant personality running roughshod over her wants and needs—

though clever Valentine still finds ways to be subversive ... as wise and witty (and stubborn) Princesses do.

Valentine's role can also be seen as the Fairy Godmother, protector, guiding Ender back from dark paths. In fairy tales, she would be the mother on whose grave grows the magic tree from which the birds toss Cinderella her dresses of gold and silver. The mother who gives her handkerchief to the Goose Girl with three drops of her blood on it, to guard her. Valentine protects Ender from Peter after his monitor is removed. She pulls Ender back from the edge with her Graff-imposed letter to him at Battle School. Most importantly, she is the glue that keeps Ender from coming apart at the psychological seams.

Valentine's heart is her weakness, but it is also her strength. Those of us who look into the mirror and see Valentine should value that strength at the same time we polish our armor, to protect not just others but also ourselves from those who would take our power away.

Peter

"You're not the smartest, Peter, just the biggest."
—VALENTINE

Ah, Peter, the Wicked King.

Peter begins his life in *Ender's Game* as the boy in fairy tales destined for greatness through hard work. He is the eldest son, the prince destined to rule the kingdom after his father. He is a natural leader, aware from a very young age of his privilege and his responsibilities.

In all of these ways, Peter Wiggin fits the criteria. He is the oldest of the Wiggin siblings, and his intelligence is on par with Valentine and Ender's. And though he eventually becomes, as the Hegemon, a good leader (or so we are told), the young Peter's loyalty is not to others but to himself. So instead of being a Prince Charming, Peter steps sideways into the role of the Wicked King—the male version of the Evil Stepmother.

The Wicked King uses others as pawns, always twelve steps ahead but only concerned with how events ultimately benefit himself and his goals. (When they launched their secret identities as Demosthenes and Locke, Valentine might have believed that there was still "a long way between writing a newsnet column and ruling the world," but in his mind, Peter was already Hegemon.) The Wicked King acts from jealousy, as Peter does from jealousy of Ender, and uses his authority selfishly, for both greater power and revenge.

Each of us experiences a taste of our own power at some point, as well as the knowledge that the potential for darkness lies within us. It's important to be aware of our own power. But it is just as important to be aware of our potential to abuse that power.

When we are threatened, we must decide: Do we take the high road or lower ourselves to the level of our enemy?

Peter is the Darth Vader of the piece, the character we fear becoming. After all, with only a small twist in his intentions, even Ender (as he well knows) has the potential to become Peter, just as Snow White turns cruel at the end of her tale and forces the wicked queen to dance in red-hot iron shoes at her wedding. But what we also learn from Peter is that, even if we've made the wrong choice in the past, it is never too late to redeem ourselves. Looking into the mirror and seeing a vision of Peter in ourselves, like Ender did, should be a reminder of that.

Welcome to Fairyland

"Me? I'm nothing. I'm a fart in the air conditioning."
—MICK

Bruno Bettelheim, a scholar who delved into the psychology of fairy tales in his book *The Uses of Enchantment*, realized that at different points in a person's life, that person had a different favorite fairy tale. The tale they identified with spoke volumes about that person's current problems, triumphs, and stage of development.

Depending on when in our lives we read *Ender's Game* and *Ender's Shadow*, we, the readers, look into that mirror and see one—or all—of Card's cast staring back at us. Are you Ender, the hero? Are you Bean, the witty Trickster? Are you gentle Princess Valentine or Valentine in her Fairy Godmother garb? Do you have a tendency to turn into Wicked King Peter?

Back when I was twelve, after my first reading of *Ender's Game*, I was unapologetically Ender, the genius child singled out and forced to follow a path not of my own choosing (my parents did not approve of my writing pursuits, so I majored in chemistry).

In college and afterwards, I was absolutely Bean. I had all of this brilliance at my disposal and no clear idea of what to do with it, but I had to make my own path with my head held high. I screwed up (a lot) and I learned (a lot) and I sacrificed (a lot) to get to be the writer I am now.

Nowadays, I feel most like Valentine, and not just because I call myself a princess. I have a family I love, a card that suddenly trumps all others—including that writing life I've shed blood, sweat, and tears for.

And yes, I could have been Peter. Not easily, but there were times in my life that I needed to be selfish, and I tapped into that dark power. Desperate times call for desperate measures...and a whole bunch of bridges to be rebuilt in the aftermath.

As young readers, we can decide who we are (Ender, Bean) and who we want to be (Valentine) and who we don't (Peter). But the characters discussed here are not, of course, the only characters in the Enderverse. As we grow and mature, we can look to see who we've become—Graff, perhaps, or Sister Carlotta. One day I may look into the Enderverse mirror and see Ender's parents staring back at me or Mazer Rackham. I think I would like to be Mazer Rackham.

When I attended his Literary Boot Camp in 2003, Orson Scott Card told me that using a mirror to describe my character physically was a cheap trick. (He was right, of course. I may have been a newbie, but I knew better.) But using one to describe your *reader*? Nothing short of brilliant.

So, open your book. Here's the mirror. It feels a little odd saying this without a giant mushroom or a hookah or a caterpillar present, but...who are *you*?

New York Times *bestselling author* **Alethea Kontis** *is a princess, a goddess, a force of nature, and a mess. She is the co-author of Sherrilyn Kenyon's* Dark-Hunter Companion *and penned the* AlphaOops *series of picture books. Her collaborations with Eisner-winning artist J.K. Lee include* The Wonderland Alphabet *and* Diary of a Mad Scientist Garden Gnome. *Her debut YA fairy-tale novel,* Enchanted, *won the Gelett Burgess Children's Book Award in 2012.*

Born in Burlington, Vermont, Alethea now lives in Northern Virginia with her Fairy Godfamily. You can find Princess Alethea online at www.aletheakontis.com.

Q. When you wrote *Ender's Game*, was the character Bean as developed in your mind as we saw him in *Ender's Shadow*?

Why did you not develop Bean's character more, especially his brilliance, in *Ender's Game*? Did you know that you were going to develop him in the Shadow series?

When I read *Ender's Game* now, it's difficult to relate the Bean from that book with the Bean we're shown throughout the Shadow series. It seems like he was never originally intended to be such an important and influential character. How hard was it to re-create the story from a new perspective when the character you were writing was more than he seemed in the first book?

A. These are easy questions to answer: I had no idea of Bean's character when I wrote *Ender's Game*. You are absolutely right that in *Ender's Game* he was never intended to be so important or interesting.

Bean grew out of the writing of *Ender's Shadow*, and by the time I got to the scenes that overlap with *Ender's Game*, the *Ender's Game* versions of the scenes were hopelessly wrong. My official excuse now is that Bean is depicted in *Ender's Game* as he seemed to that novel's point-of-view character; minor characters in one story are the heroes of their own tales. But the real cause of these discrepancies is that I came to know Bean (or, to be correct, successfully invented Bean) as a much more complex character than it was possible or desirable to make him when telling Ender's story.

—*OSC*

Q. Why did you feel a need to continue on with Bean's story rather than the other characters in *Ender's Game*?

A. The original plan was to collaborate with other writers, allowing them to create books about several characters from Ender's team. When Neal Shusterman was talking with me about which character he'd like to write about, he chose Bean, and I agreed with him that Bean had the most potential of any of the other Battle School kids. But the truth is that *none* of the Battle School kids was particularly well developed in the original novel; only Petra, Bean, and Dink showed real possibilities, and Bean most of all because he was the character seen by Ender as most like himself.

Though the economics of Neal writing a book about Bean made the collaboration impractical, I was by then committed to the idea of such a book existing; the economics worked fine if I wrote the book myself. (The adage is, "Collaboration is twice the work for half the money.") In the process of creating the whole Shadow series, however, I found myself writing the stories of *all* the Battle School kids, including several that we never actually met in *Ender's Game*. So instead of having a Bean novel, then a Petra novel, then a Dink novel, and so on, I wrote the five Shadow novels as an answer to the question, "What happened to all the Battle School kids after the war?" structured around Bean's life.

—OSC

SIZE MATTERS

JANIS IAN

1. The necessary disclaimers

Let me start by saying that I'm short.

Not *diminutive* or *petite* but *short*. Four feet, ten-and-a-quarter inches worth of short, to be exact. Just a quarter-inch past tall enough to qualify for the United States Air Force.

I read years ago that the height limit to designate a person as a dwarf or midget was a quarter inch lower than my own height. That only bothered me when I thought my size might help me get a college scholarship. Apparently, in this one instance, I was not short enough. But no one would ever mistake me for *tall* or even *average height*. By any current measurement, I am short.

I know Orson Scott Card. I have pictures of myself standing next to him. Scott is far from short. Why he chose to write a book that not only makes lack of height an asset but comes close to glorifying it is beyond me.

Nevertheless, I thank him profusely for it.

2. Does size really matter?

Of course it does. Anyone my size who's tried to adjust a showerhead, use a hotel magnifying mirror, or pull clothes out of the top dryer knows that. The world is not set up for short people. Kitchen counters are too high, causing wrist and shoulder problems for those of us who like to cook. Chairs are too tall, cutting off circulation mid-thigh and leading to stiff legs at best, phlebitis at worst.

Forget rental cars; those seats are designed for the Los Angeles Lakers. Forget seatbelts, for that matter. I can never decide whether I'd rather risk being thrown through the car window in an accident, or having my trachea crushed by a seatbelt designed for someone at least a foot above my height.

And that's just the physical aspect. Let's talk perception.

When someone comments, "He's really tall!" it summons up images of power, masculinity, success. The equating of size with dominance is consistent throughout the known world. And *lack* of stature is associated with lack of intelligence and competence, leading people to treat someone my height as though he or she were, in fact, a large child rather than a tiny adult. I am often patted on the head by new acquaintances, who seem to regard me as a benign sheepdog, but without the drool.

In David Henry Hwang's marvelous play *M. Butterfly*, a diplomat called Rene Gallimard is posted to China. A typical colonialist, he refuses to learn anything about the culture and, because of that, is easily blind sided by the cultural differences between East and West.

One night, he attends the Peking Opera, where he is completely enraptured by Song Liling, an actress with the company. They meet, at his insistence, and spend time together. In his eyes, the petite Song is tentative and shy, longing to be conquered. Or rather, to be dominated.

To Gallimard, the East—so backward, so barbaric, so filled with miniature people who can't *really* be serious about politics or diplomacy—secretly longs to be conquered by the West. And as is always the case, arrogance and ignorance combine to create a huge blind spot, which plays right into Song's hands. She parlays his paternalism into an affair, gaining access to state secrets in the process.

The spineless, colorless Gallimard is close to the bottom of his profession. However, as the affair with Song Liling continues, his ascendancy over her provokes a heady sense of power. He becomes more "manlike," more forceful, more demanding in the other areas of his life, and that empowerment actually enables him to begin rising through the ranks of the diplomatic service.

Onstage, Song is small, especially when standing next to Gallimard. As an audience, we equate her size with fragility and weakness. She uses her size to cultivate an air of simpering incompetence whenever Gallimard is near. She seems unable to make choices for herself; she asks his help constantly. She *needs* a man like Gallimard, a big man, one who will protect her and make decisions for her.

Midway through M. *Butterfly*, there is an intermission. Those of us who remain seated watch Song as she seats herself at a makeup table facing the audience. The table's "mirror" is empty space, allowing us to watch as she removes first her makeup, then her wig, then her kimono, and finally, her very gender.

We discover in that moment that Song is, in fact, male.

In the original Broadway production I saw, B. D. Wong played Song and John Lithgow was Gallimard. The difference in height was striking. For the entire first half of the play, we watched as Lithgow towered over the fragile and feminine Wong, who swayed and sashayed and seduced as we willingly went along with the caricature of femininity.

Inevitably, Song Liling is exposed as a spy and Gallimard as her willing dupe. He is put on trial, but even as the evidence mounts, he refuses to believe she is male. Never mind the question of hidden homosexuality here—that's not the point. Gallimard cannot believe that someone so delicate, so perceptive, so adoring, could possibly share his genital makeup. She made him feel like a giant, and he cannot let go of that without returning to his former barren state.

As Song says, addressing the court: "The West thinks of itself as masculine—big guns, big industry, big money—so the East is feminine—weak, delicate, poor...but good at art, and full of inscrutable wisdom—the feminine mystique...The West believes the East, deep down, *wants* to be dominated—because a woman can't think for herself."

Early in the play, Gallimard's refusal to learn about Chinese culture, the arrogance of insisting he *knows*, spills over into a disastrous conversation with his ambassador, who asks Gallimard's opinion about China's involvement in Viet Nam. Flush with a lover's courage, Gallimard insists the Orient will always bow to a superior force, so the Americans must continue to show strength. This is his brilliant political analysis. Western victory over the East is inevitable because the East isn't really serious, can't really be a threat. He makes the mistake of assuming physical size is congruent with mental, and emotional, size.

So it is with us and children.

3. Size is in the eye of the beholder

We underestimate children. Their lack of stature leads us to assume they're innocent, although there's really no reason to believe that. If anything, they are often more vicious, and more cunning, than adults. It's difficult for a child to see the big picture, especially a six-year-old child. No matter how bright, he lacks the life experience of spending time with many different people, of different backgrounds and ages, in dissimilar situations.

Children know very little of long-term consequence. They don't think that far ahead. The boy who, having seen the Roadrunner cartoon a zillion times, pushes his small friend off a cliff, fully expecting the friend to bounce back, doesn't have the experience to make the leap from cartoon to reality. And Ender, who *does* normally think days and weeks and years ahead of everyone else, is too exhausted and broken apart when he's made to play the final "game" to understand that all this time, it's been no game at all, that his commands have sent real men and women to their deaths.

A writer I know insists that the across-the-board, age-defiant success of *Ender's Game* is because the publisher has marketed it so cleverly. He says once the book "lost its legs" in the adult science fiction market, its clever publisher somehow turned it into a young adult novel, then managed to insinuate it into thousands of required high school reading lists.

Balderdash. The reason *Ender's Game* succeeds with all age groups, outside of the obvious something-for-everyone, is that it shatters assumptions. From the first, we know that Ender and his siblings are incredibly bright. When he enters Battle School, we meet a nation of children so smart that we'd find their intelligence level impossible to accept—except Card also makes them incredibly young, and for the most part (particularly in Ender's case), very, very small.

That their exceptional intelligence is what makes them good soldiers is a lot easier to swallow than the idea that their age or size makes them more capable of fighting, and winning, a war than we adults are. The contrast between their age and their capabilities assists us in a massive suspension of disbelief; the children's intelligence almost seems credible by comparison.

What does that do to us as readers?

We are used to thinking of words like *up* and *tall* as associated with good things. Academics are expected to speak an *elevated* tongue. Phrases like *small-minded* and *short-tempered* are used to denigrate.

We *look down* on someone we disapprove of, and we *look up* to someone we admire. We have *lofty* ideas, and *walk tall* when we're proud of ourselves. *Up* is always better than *down*, and *the sky's the limit* sounds much more poetic to us than *the core of the Earth's the limit!*

Even Amazon.com uses height to denote safety and trustworthiness. They've done a wonderful job of convincing people like my partner, normally a hard-nosed defense attorney, that their data is safely stored somewhere in the stratosphere. They call it *The Cloud*, and by calling it that instead of *a bunch of servers somewhere off the coast of Greenland*, they make us into linguistic fools. Think of the images *cloud* brings to mind: Sweet dreams. Soft pillows. Gentle light. Angels, wings outstretched, playing harps while floating gently above a billowy cloud. And above all that, heaven. The place where God himself chooses to live.

Surely my data will be safe there, up on high!

With *Ender's Game*, Card insists we throw the concepts of *high* and *low* out the window. He forces our relationship with these undersized young humans into a *quid pro quo* between equals. No, not even between equals, because none of the adults can do what Ender and his compatriots can do—*the children* are the heroes of the tale. The adults are merely guides, and occasional torturers, who manage to spend a great deal of their time getting in Ender's way and almost ruining everything.

When Ender says, "The enemy's gate is down," we enter an alternate universe, where *up* is relative and *down* is where you must go to win the game. Up and down become malleable concepts in *Ender's Game*, as does size. Being short is only a problem relative to the bigger kid who might want to beat you up because he may have an arm's length advantage.

But even then, being short gives you speed and the element of surprise.

What a reversal!

4. Size in *Ender's Game* and *Ender's Shadow*

In the original book, Ender is described as *small* twenty-eight times. When I added the adjective *little* to my search, only when used as a height descriptor, it made for a total of seventy-two references to Ender's diminutive stature.

That's a lot of *short*.

Ender isn't the only short one. All the Battle School launchies are. Of course they are! They're five, six, seven years old. Even Stilson, the bully Ender kills, "wasn't bigger than most other kids, but he was bigger than Ender." (Later in the book, Card writes, "He dreamed that night of Stilson, only he saw now how small Stilson was, only six years old, how ridiculous his tough-guy posturing was…" Even Ender, as he grows out of childhood, begins to see their size as absurd.)

Card constantly reminds us of Ender's short stature. He even shows us, through Ender's encounter with his first desk, how awful it must be to reach full size:

> Ender spread his hands over the child-size keyboard near the edge of the desk and wondered what it would feel like to have hands as large as a grownup's. They must feel so big and awkward, thick stubby fingers and beefy palms. Of course, they had bigger keyboards—but how could their thick fingers draw a fine line, the way Ender could, a thin

line so precise that he could make it spiral seventy-nine times from the center to the edge of the desk without the lines ever touching or overlapping.

In *Ender's Game*, maturing, attaining your full size, means you're out of the game.

Though Ender is tiny, Bean, who becomes the closest thing to a best friend Ender will have, is still tinier: "Ender was still small for a commander. His feet didn't come near the end of the bunk. There was plenty of room for Bean to curl up at the foot of the bed. So he climbed up and then lay still, so as not to disturb Ender's sleep" (*Ender's Shadow*).

For Bean, raised on the streets, left to live by his own wits from the first, his size is an asset. He survived the attack on the laboratory where he was born only because he was small enough to hide in a toilet tank. Later, he's still small enough to fit into the air vents that run through the Battle School, small enough to move through them silently. He worries about the day when he'll be too big to fit, unable to overhear conversations or see passwords as teachers enter them on their private keyboards. Again, maturity, attaining full size, moves you out of the power position and into the unknown.

Throughout the series, the formics are referred to as *buggers*. What an interesting play on words! *Bugs* are small, annoying insects. They dart in and out, stinging and biting and mostly causing us to itch—not exactly a death threat. It's a rare (visible) bug that causes life-threatening damage.

The formics tower over their human counterparts. Calling them *buggers* at once negates their size and renders them harmless. Sort of like changing *Chinese* to *Chink*, which is a small crack in a wall that can easily be fixed with a little cement.

Interestingly enough, the weapon that ends the Formic War is called the Little Doctor. It's a horrific weapon of mass destruction. It feeds on the energy of that which it destroys, creating a ping-pong effect, and eventually obliterates not just formics and ships but entire planets. There is nothing left of them.

The Little Doctor doesn't only destroy the formic race; it wipes out their history, their cultural record. It removes them from the memory of the universe, denying them any chance ever to speak for themselves. It destroys their past and, therefore, their future.

What a terrible device.

Ender wonders at the name, and Mazer Rackham explains the derivation. He tells Ender that the device was originally known as a *Molecular Detachment Device—M.D. device—Dr. device*. Ender doesn't quite get the joke. Destruction on that scale isn't funny to him, and he isn't old enough to see the black humor of it, or that it's a way of whistling in the dark.

Even though Rackham clarifies *Doctor*, the term *Little* is never explained. Is it part of the description just because soldiers like to name their weapons?[1] Because something so big must be made small before the human mind can cope

---

[1] It could also be a reference to Little Boy, the atomic bomb dropped on Hiroshima, named "Little" in contrast to the other two WWII bomb design projects.

with its existence, let alone its usage? We're never told. We are left instead to assume that the description *Little Doctor* is not so much illustrative as affectionate. The bomb as friend and ally, cut down to size.

5. Where gratitude comes in

If it weren't for this article, I would never have researched size. And if it weren't for my research, I would not be convinced, as I am now, that I will live much longer than most of the tall people I've envied all my life.

It's those darned telomeres.

Telomeres are little tails at the end of our chromosomes that keep them from unraveling. Our cells have to refresh themselves constantly by duplicating, so the old cell can die and the new one can take over its duties. Each time a cell duplicates itself, the telomeres at the end of the chromosomes get shorter. When they get too short, the cell loses its ability to duplicate.

You've heard how, every seven years, all the cells in your body are replaced and brand new? Well, sooner or later all good things must come to an end. The reason the functional capacity of vital organs declines as we get older is that those damaged cells can't be replaced.

Many years ago, a fellow named Hayflick showed that most human cells have only a limited capacity for duplication. Larger people need a larger number of duplications to replace defective or dead cells as they age.[2] In theory, the

---

[2] *Bulletin of the World Health Organization*, 1992.

fewer times a cell has to duplicate itself, the longer the body can last.

Statistically, shorter ninety-year-olds have longer telomeres and better survival rates.[3] Studies of healthy centenarians show that they have longer telomeres than centenarians in poor health.[4] In a study of geriatric Swedes, shorter humans were shown to have a lower mortality rate. In fact, the study showed a loss of 0.52 years per centimeter of height increase.[5] (If it's true that we lose almost half a year of life for every extra centimeter of growth, it would go a long way toward explaining why women seem to outlive men no matter what other factors come into play.)

Our various organs are pretty much the same size from human to human. At four feet, ten inches my heart is about as big as that of a person who is six feet, five inches. But his heart is going to have to work a lot harder than mine to pump blood through his frame, keep him upright and

---

[3] Andrea B. Maier, Diana van Heemst, and Rudi G. J. Westendorp, "Relation between Body Height & Replicative Capacity of Human Fibroblasts in Nonagenarians," in the *Journal of Gerontology*, http://biomedgerontology.oxfordjournals.org/content/63/1/43.full.

[4] Dellara F. Terry, Vikki G. Nolan, Stacy L. Andersen, et al., "Association of Longer Telomeres With Better Health in Centenarians," in the *Journal of Gerontology: Biological Sciences*, http://www.nia.nih.gov/health/publication/biology-aging.

[5] Jesse C. Krakauer MD, Barry Franklin PhD, Michael Kleerekoper MD, Magnus Karlsson MD, PhD, James A. Levine MD, PhD, "Body Composition Profiles Derived From Dual-Energy X-Ray Absorptiometry, Total Body Scan, and Mortality," in *Preventive Cardiology*, http://onlinelibrary.wiley.com/doi/10.1111/j.1520-037X.2004.3326.x/full.

moving, even help him take a deep breath. The longer and harder you use a pump, the sooner it wears out.

But wait! There's more!

Shorter people are less likely to require surgery for her niated spinal disks, less likely to break a hip from falling, less likely to die in auto crashes.[6]

And it's not just about length of life or health—it's about the planet. A decrease of just ten pounds in the average weight of a US citizen would decrease airline fuel consumption by 350 million gallons yearly!

So if you think about it, I'm really doing the rest of you a favor by being this short. Even if, nowadays, they give children like me hormones to make sure we don't stay this way.

6. Psyche and substance

In his new book, *Short: Walking Tall When You Are Not Tall At All*, Jonathan Schwartz (five feet, three inches tall) of the *New York Times* argues forcefully that it is drug companies marketing growth hormones who insist being short is somehow a disadvantage. To hear the hormone-pushers tell it, allowing your less-than-average-height children to remain that way will ruin their future. This attitude has become pervasive as the world continues to connect height with quality.

Schwartz argues that, rather than being a drawback, shortness builds character. His thought is further backed up by author Stephen Hall, who said in a recent interview:

---

[6] Thomas T. Samaras, *Human Body Size & the Laws of Scaling: Physiological, Performance, Growth, Longevity and Ecological Ramifications.*

One of Darwin's most astonishing evolutionary insights is the suggestion that humans, precisely because they were smaller and weaker than their primate cousins, evolved the skills of social cooperation that have made us the successful species we are today.[7]

In other words, being short, especially during the teen years, may force a child to become perceptive, aware, and socially intelligent. Certainly, this is true of Ender Wiggin. His intelligence and will to succeed make him an obvious target for bullies and fools. But his size gives him an edge they can't duplicate, emotionally and physiologically.

Over and over again, being the runt forces Ender to find ways in and out of situations using his brain and his wit, rather than bludgeoning his way through. Of all the commanders, only Ender sees that allowing those under him to make their own decisions in battle is the only way for him to win all the time. Ender is the only commander capable of completely setting ego aside in order to become part of the social cooperative. Had he been normally sized, able to use brawn instead of brain to get his way, it would have been very different. He might have had an outsized ego instead, and that ego would never have allowed him to form his toons into "separate but equal" groups.

Ender is exceptional, not in spite of his size but because of it. And because Card is kind enough not to assign

---

[7] Stephen Hall (author of *Size Matters: How Height Affects the Health, Happiness, and Success of Boys—and the Men they Become*) in a 2010 *Talk of the Nation* interview.

a specific height to Ender at any future point, we can continue to see him in our mind's eye as small, lithe, quick on his feet, and incredibly perceptive and honorable to boot—things he might not have had to become if he'd always been *average*.

7. In short...

Breeding for size used to be important. People needed big, strong children to work the fields, fend off dangerous predators, and beat out the neighboring tribe for healthy spouses and the best land. But now, with the rise of *geek* and *nerd* as terms of not just affection but downright approbation, size isn't nearly as essential. In fact, in a lot of respects it's quite the opposite, not only inessential but destructive to the planet.

Shorter people have less impact on the environment—we require less food, less air, less water. A 10 percent reduction in height, worldwide, would lead to a commensurate reduction in everything from beef and pork consumption (and their attending methane problems) to highway congestion. And if we keep insisting that taller is better, we may eventually grow ourselves right out of living on the planet, and into six feet under—if we can still fit.

There are a lot of upsides to being small. Short people have a lower center of gravity, which creates greater stability overall. We make good gymnasts, jockeys, car racers, figure skaters—anything that requires speed coupled with dexterity and balance. We're lower to the ground, which means we don't have as far to rise when we fall.

We live longer. If you don't want to bother struggling through all the scientific data I cited, just think about dogs. Small dogs live longer. Everybody knows that.

We're beneficial to society as a whole. From Harriet Tubman and Danny DeVito (five feet each) and Mae West (five feet, one inch) to Beethoven, Picasso, and James Madison (all under five feet, four inches), we are everywhere. We're over-represented in the arts, in politics, in the sciences. We win our wars, both social and political, through cunning and cleverness rather than brute force, just as Ender does. And we happily claim him as one of our own.

While hunting around online for information on size, telomeres, and random DNA mutations, I happened upon various lists teenagers made to express why they felt good about being short. Here are just a few:

You can duck faster.

There's less chance of being struck by lightning.

You're always in the front of group pictures.

You can get up faster when you fall down.

You can fit into cool cars.

There's less chance of being hit by a UFO.

And my personal favorite:

You can fit into places like a locker to hide from bullies. Granted you are also small enough to get stuffed in one, but that's a chance I am willing to take.

There's also this quote by boxer Joe Walcott, a quote so true it's entered into the lexicon:

The bigger they are, the harder they fall.

And that about sums it up.

Janis Ian is a songwriter's songwriter who began writing songs at twelve years of age and performed onstage at New York's Village Gate just one year later. Her first record, Society's Child, was released two years after that. The seminal At Seventeen brought her five of her nine Grammy nominations, and songs like "Jesse" and "Some People's Lives" have been recorded by artists as diverse as Celine Dion, John Mellencamp, Mel Tormé, Glen Campbell, and Bette Midler. Tina Fey even named a character "Janis Ian" in her movie Mean Girls!

Janis' energy does not stop at performing. Her autobiography, Society's Child, a starred Booklist review and Publisher's Weekly pick (and now also available as an audio book), details her life and career. The audiobook recently brought her ninth Grammy nomination, in the Best Spoken Word category, alongside ex-President Bill Clinton, Michelle Obama, Rachel Maddow, and Ellen Degeneres. Her song "Stars" is also the title of an anthology featuring twenty-four major science fiction writers, all of them "tipping the hat" by writing original stories based on songs Janis wrote that affected their own lives.

Janis runs The Pearl Foundation, named for her mother, and has raised over $700,000 for scholarships for returning students at various universities and colleges.

More information can be found at her website, www.janisian.com.

Q. Did the pilots and soldiers who were a part of the Third Invasion know beforehand that they were led by kids? How did they react initially?

A. This is a question that I did not answer definitively even in my own mind, going back and forth on it while writing both the short story "Ender's Game" and the novel *Ender's Game*. It is hard to remember now which way I decided at the time; what is certain is that I tried to dodge the issue completely in the novel.

The question really came down to this: When Ender's subordinates—his "jeesh," as I named them when I wrote *Ender's Shadow*—gave orders to the squadrons under their control, were they doing so orally or electronically?

They were certainly *not* taking command of individual ships, as if they were piloting them in a videogame. The "simulation" they were "playing" was a command simulator, not a combat simulator. This was Command School, so their "training" was in giving orders to groups and individuals who would then carry out the commands.

The children would believe that, in showing them the actions of the squadrons they commanded, the computer was simulating the normal variances in human behavior—commands misunder-stood, orders exceeded, or pilots who took individual initiative as the situation developed in unpredicted ways.

If the children gave commands elec-tronically, then the pilots could remain unaware that children were command-ing them. The orders would come onto a screen, and their responses would return the same way—rather like texting. The trouble with such a system is how slowly it goes. I could imagine a menu of pre-typed orders, rather like a McDonald's cash register—but that would mean that at moments when surprising, unpredict-able orders were most urgently needed, such a command system would require that the commander shift to the much slower method of typing.

This gave preference, then, to oral commands. Human speech has evolved to be by far our most convenient com-munication method. You can speak an order and receive it without removing your visual attention from the screens and gauges you have to keep observing. We know this because we carry on con-versations while driving cars; and, unlike actors in movies, we do *not* turn to look at each other during such conversations. We keep our eyes on the road, because we cannot afford to remove our visual at-tention from developing situations as we move forward.

It is possible to imagine some kind of voice-disguise system, or a translation from voice to text and then back again. But as I worked with producer Lynn Hendee on my versions of the movie script, we realized that any system that put a filter between the kids and the men they were commanding would be counterproductive. There needed to be at least one-way clarity. That is, the men would need to hear the voices of the children, for the sake of immediacy and quickness of response. Yet the children could never be allowed to hear the voices of the men they commanded, or they would know the game was real.

Thus, in the early development of the movie scripts—and before I wrote *Ender's Shadow*—I had to commit to the idea that all the men of the fleet knew they were being commanded by children.

How, then, could they be reconciled with this? Ultimately, this would not be hard. Their voyage took fifty years (though they experienced it as only two years, because of near-lightspeed time contraction and dilation effects). Before they left, they were fully informed that their commander in every battle would be the *same* person, communicating with them by ansible from IF-COM, the International Fleet headquarters on Eros.

They assumed that it would be Mazer Rackham, or, perhaps, a better commander who was trained and discovered after they left. They assumed that if it was not Mazer, who was being kept alive by a closed-loop near-lightspeed voyage of his own, it would be someone born later, probably someone born after they left the solar system. After all, someone born the day they left would be fifty by the time they reached their destinations—all the known formic planets.

When the battlefleets neared their targets, the only possible commander would be twelve years old. The military leaders on Eros had to decide what to tell the pilots, and when. Remember that the years of Ender's training would seem less than four months to the pilots in the fleet. So if they were to be told that children would, or might, be their commanders, it would be better to give them the news in plenty of time to get used to the idea.

There are scenes in discarded movie scripts in which we see those pilots learning about this, discussing it. But in truth it's not as if they had a choice, except the choice a soldier of any kind always has: to desert, to mutiny, to refuse to fight. And what then would their sacrifice be worth? For these men had already left behind all their families and communities. If they were victorious, if they ever returned to Earth, it would be a hundred years since their departure. Everyone they knew would long be dead. And if they refused to obey whatever orders they were given, what then? Where would they go? Their fighters could not make inter-stellar voyages at near-lightspeed. They had nowhere to go.

No, they would accept what they had to accept. But their commanders, not being fools—or at least *trying* not to be fools, for fools rarely suspect themselves of foolishness—would do all they could to sweeten the situation. They would show the pilots who would be taking orders from these children just how the kids had performed in the battle room, with plenty of videos. These young commanders would be more than names. They would be people.

Of course, this was pure propaganda—they would never show them moments that might cause doubt. But just because the vids were meant to persuade the pilots to accept the children did not mean that the pilots were not being told the truth. These really *were* impressive kids.

And whatever doubts remained—surely there were still many of them—were dispelled as soon as Ender and his jeesh took command in the first battle. It was an easy victory, with tactics that seemed obvious to Ender Wiggin and the other kids—but there was no reason to think the tactics would have seemed obvious to the pilots. What they would see was: victory, and few losses on the human side. Soldiers appreciate that combination.

—OSC

RETHINKING THE CHILD HERO

AARON JOHNSTON

I once heard Orson Scott Card describe Ender Wiggin as "a short Clint Eastwood." My first reaction was to laugh. Short Clint Eastwood. Ha! In my mind I envisioned Ender hovering in the Battle Room, leveling his gun at Bonzo, one side of Ender's lip curled up in a sneer, speaking in his slightly falsetto, prepubescent voice, "Go ahead, punk. Make my day."

The more I thought about this description of Ender, however, the more I realized it was no joke. Card is right. Ender *is* a short Clint Eastwood. And although Card didn't specify which version of Clint Eastwood he meant (i.e., *Dirty Harry* Clint Eastwood or Spaghetti Western Clint Eastwood or bare-knuckle-fighter-with-an-orangutan-on-his-hip Clint Eastwood, as in *Every Which Way But Loose*), it

149

really doesn't matter. Clint Eastwood plays himself in all his movies anyway. The only differences between *Dirty Harry* Clint Eastwood and Spaghetti Western Clint Eastwood are concrete and a bigger gun.

But I digress. The point is, Ender Wiggin is a lot like every character Clint Eastwood has ever played, all of whom seem to live by the same code:

1. Talk little.
2. Observe everything.
3. Know your enemy.
4. Win.

Ender would likely revise number three to "Know *and love* your enemy," and we would allow him this edit. His compassion is probably the biggest difference between him and the venerable Mr. Eastwood. Allow me to illustrate.

Picture in your mind the poncho-wearing, Spaghetti Western Clint Eastwood, with his itchy trigger finger ready, and his eyes half-closed in that Mexican standoff stare, and a dead vaquero at his feet, bleeding out in the dirt. If you were to approach Clint and say, "Mr. Eastwood, I know you must feel awful about killing this man. He is the last sweaty vaquero of his kind. Here, I found this silky cocoon. Inside is an infant sweaty vaquero. Take it and find a place for it out in the desert where it can break free of its cocoon and flourish." Then you would hand the cocoon to Clint Eastwood, whereupon he would throw it up into the air and blast it to hell with his six-shooter.

So yes, Clint and Ender have their differences. But that shouldn't keep us from noting their many similarities. Both are independent. Both are gunslingers. Both are quick to defend the bullied and oppressed. Both are cool as cucumbers and rarely show their emotions. Both are swift and lethal. Both are wanderers—Ender becomes one after being exiled. Both speak only when necessary and say only what needs to be said. And, perhaps most importantly, both are white knights, or killers with hearts of gold. Even Clint Eastwood. In *The Good, the Bad, and the Ugly*, he's the Good.

And did you notice that Orson Scott Card described Ender as a *short* Clint Eastwood and not as a *young* Clint Eastwood? There's a difference. To call Ender a *young* Clint Eastwood is to suggest that Ender has the seed of heroism within him, that slowly over time he will grow up and become a true hero. But to say that Ender is a *short* Clint Eastwood is to say that Ender is a hero now, as he is, as a child. Or in other words, Ender is as much a hero as any adult hero.

That's significant. In fact, when the short story version of *Ender's Game* was first published in 1977, the idea that a child could be equal to an adult in terms of intelligence or talent or capabilities was somewhat revolutionary. Up until then, children in fiction were generally weaker, less intelligent, less introspective, less insightful, and less emotionally complex than adults. As evidence, simply ask yourself: What child in fiction prior to 1977 could be described as a short Clint Eastwood? Or a short Hercules? Or a short General Patton? Or a short anyone? How many child characters displayed the skills and attributes and intelligence of their taller counterparts?

I doubt many characters spring to mind.

However, if I were to ask you that same question about the child heroes in fiction today, I suspect you could name quite a few. Harry Potter, Artemis Fowl, Lyra Belacqua, Percy Jackson, Eragon, and the list goes on and on. These children, like Ender before them, are all heroes in the classical and mythic sense. Rather than stand idly by while the adults solve all the problems and make all the decisions, these modern-day child heroes take the helm, defeat evil, and prove time and again that they have the same capacity for greatness that adults do.

Ender's Game helped pave that road. Card emphatically declares through young Ender Wiggin that children are people too—capable, intelligent, heroic people. Not bumbling, naïve fairy-tale heroes like Hansel and Gretel, but real heroes. Smart and cunning and unstoppable. Mythic heroes in every sense.

The Mythic Hero

In his book *The Hero with a Thousand Faces*, Joseph Campbell suggests that the adventures of mythic heroes all follow the same formula, a story structure he calls the monomyth. Pick any hero you like, from Perseus to Luke Skywalker, and you can plug the steps of that hero's adventure into this mythic structure. It's not scientific, of course. Not every hero myth is identical. Sometimes the steps may be in a different order or missing from the pattern entirely. Campbell says that's the point. The monomyth isn't an architectural blueprint. It's a skeletal structure that can be skinned a thousand different ways.

Ender's Game, it turns out, fits the structure quite well. Take a look-see.

Campbell dissects the monomyth into three steps: (1) separation (2) initiation and (3) return. During separation, the hero receives a call to adventure that requires him to leave the ordinary world he knows and enter a world of supernatural wonder. In Ender's case, this means leaving his family and entering Battle School, a world of zero gravity and games and social structures all completely foreign to Ender.

During initiation, the hero must immerse himself in the new world. He must learn rules, gain allies, confront rivals, and overcome a series of trials. It's not easy. The hero will be challenged, attacked, and deceived. He will face danger and disgrace. Forces will combine against him. His tasks will require exceptional talent or skill. (Hmm. Sounds like the brochure copy for Battle School, doesn't it?)

After the hero's immersion into the world, the hero must enter the figurative inmost cave, face death, and slay a powerful enemy, an event Campbell calls the Supreme Ordeal. This is not the final battle for the hero but rather a precursor to it. The experience forever changes the hero and prepares him for the ultimate confrontation yet to come.

In Ender's case, the inmost cave is the steaming hot shower, and the enemy is Bonzo. Their battle is a shocking ordeal that crushes Ender emotionally and, ultimately, prepares him for his final showdown with the formics.

It is also during this initiation phase that the hero meets a powerful goddess who is, according to *The Hero with a Thousand Faces*, "mother, sister, mistress, bride," and who often comes to the hero in "the deep of sleep." She is the "world creatrix, ever mother...the life of everything that lives. The death of everything that dies."

In *Ender's Game*, this goddess is of course the hive queen. She is literally the life of all formics, the queen mother, the memory-holder, the queen-body as well as all the workers. Without her, the formics cannot survive. She is their life and their death. And she comes to Ender during this stage through the mind game and in his dreams, swimming through his psyche and examining his heart. Ender doesn't know that his dreams and gameplay are influenced by the hive queen. That isn't revealed until much later in *Xenocide*, long after Ender has discovered the cocoon and he and the hive queen have formed a strong philotic bond. But the significance of these initial connections with the hive queen cannot be overstated. They are the beginning of Ender's journey toward greater enlightenment.

That enlightenment is ultimately achieved in the final phase of the hero's journey: the return. Following the hero's initiation, he must face the final enemy and slay them in hand-to-hand combat. Then, once that victory is won, the hero earns a great reward, which he then must take back with him to the ordinary world and share with others, thus giving to them the same enlightenment that he himself has achieved.

Ender is a unique case here because, after facing the formics, he doesn't physically return to the ordinary world. He can't, he's exiled. Yet even so, Ender still fits the pattern of the mythic hero because he inevitably shares his reward with the ordinary world. He brings them enlightenment, even in his absence.

His reward is actually two things: the formic cocoon and the wisdom and enlightenment he gains from the formics when he sees into the mind of the hive queen and finally understands them. The cocoon is a reward because it is the answer to Ender's psychological burden. He has committed xenocide, and the grief and guilt he feels as a result are almost unbearable. With the cocoon he can restore the formic species and undo the wrong he has committed. Ender doesn't give the cocoon to the ordinary world he left behind, but he does give it to the greater world, the universe, where in some small corner the cocoon can open and bring life anew to the formics.

The second reward, the understanding of the formics, Ender shares with the ordinary world by means of the book *The Hive Queen*, which he writes from the hive queen's perspective. The text brings enlightenment to all the world, opening their minds to who the formics really are and what their motivations were in invading Earth. As a result, the formics are no longer perceived as monsters but as "tragic sisters" of the human race.

We're only skimming the surface of the monomyth here, but it's clear to see that Ender fits the pattern of the mythic hero to the letter. He leaves the ordinary world to embark on a greater quest, immersing himself into a strange new world, wherein he finds allies and enemies and a goddess. He overcomes incredible obstacles and undergoes a Supreme Ordeal. He confronts a seemingly insurmountable enemy and uses his unique talents and skills to slay that enemy. He earns a reward and returns to the ordinary world enlightened. Does he demonstrate courage? Yes. Self-sacrifice? You betcha. Perseverance? Brilliance? Goodness? Check, check, and check. He's a mythic hero in every sense. Considering how child heroes were represented in the past, that's a bigger deal than you might think.

Child Heroes of Yore

Prior to *Ender's Game*, most child heroes in fiction were passive participants in their own stories. They were the victims, the ragamuffins, the tagalongs, the observers of the action, the character strolling through the magical realm, doing little more than soaking in the world around her (e.g., *Alice in Wonderland*). They were the people being acted upon, not the ones driving the action.

Or, if they *were* taking a more active role, they were usually doing so only with other children. If they governed, they governed other children. If they outsmarted someone, they outsmarted other children. The class system between children and adults was in force. Think *Lord of the Flies* or *The Great Brain* or the Encyclopedia Brown adventures. Was Encyclopedia Brown a paid consultant for the police force? No, he spent his afternoons outsmarting Bugs Meany, a neighborhood punk about his age who committed petty crimes like stealing coins from some kid's lemonade stand.

Oh sure, there were instances in which Encyclopedia implicated a real criminal in a real crime, but by and large child heroes pre–*Ender's Game* were heroes on a small scale. Their power was limited. Their reach was short. Their influence was slight. The stakes of their adventures were relatively low. And everything was coated with a glaze of childhood

innocence or giggle-inducing silliness. *Pippi Longstocking.*
Charlie and the Chocolate Factory. *Little House on the Prairie.*

Ender's Game was different. Ender wasn't weak and powerless and always playing second fiddle to adults. He was
smarter than the adults. He could do things adults couldn't.
You want him to fight two armies at once? No problem. You
want him to transform a bunch of untrained launchies into
an unbeatable army? Bring it on.

With *Ender's Game*, child heroes and our expectations
for them grew up. Children, it turns out, can do more than
return stolen coins to lemonade stands. They can also save
the world.

But rather than speak in general terms, let's look at a
few specific examples.

Consider first the young hero of *Oliver Twist.* A text-
book definition of the powerless child hero. You need not
go any farther than the title of the book to see my point.
Oliver sounds like a weak name, doesn't it? It's not Bruno
or Buck or Kirk or Drago, big husky masculine names that
put fear in a man's heart. It's Oliver. Poor, little, aw shucks
Oliver. It sounds a lot like *I'm going to walk "all over" you.*
Which of course is precisely what most of the adults in the
story do. Then there's the last name. Twist. Throughout
the story, Oliver is twisted and manhandled by adults. He's
shoved through windows to help a burglar; he's twisted and
smacked around by schoolmasters and bullies and villain-
ous adults. We should probably call him Oliver Twist My
Arm Behind My Back.

Then there's Ender Wiggin. The kid's name is Ender, for
crying out loud. That speaks volumes, doesn't it? This is the

kid who finishes what he starts. This is the guy who puts the bad guys down for good. You want to start a fight? Fine, this kid will *end* it. Kapow!

But let us go beyond the title page of both books, shall we? Consider the story of Oliver Twist. One of the most memorable scenes of the book—made famous by the musical adaptation of it—is poor orphaned Oliver, with his clothes filthy and tattered, his arms and legs as thin as twigs, shuffling helplessly up to the soup server, empty bowl outstretched, asking, "Please, sir. Can I have some more?"

Well of course you can't have any more, you little twit. Who are you to talk to an adult that way? How dare you question the portions I serve? Spank spank smack! Insolent little child. Spank spank!

Poor Ollie. Talk about the short end of the stick.

Now, compare that same scene to Orson Scott Card's version of the hungry orphan, a.k.a. Bean, a.k.a. Ender's shadow. Does Bean play the role of the powerless child hero and beg and plead an adult for more soup? No. He shows ruthless survival instincts and brilliant strategic thinking and he gets all the soup he can eat. Does he get smacked around? No, he and his crew do the smacking. He even wisely sees what Achilles truly is and gives the order to kill him. Can you see Oliver Twist doing that? Not in a million years.

Note that the defining trait of the modern-day child hero is not violence. It's initiative. It's strength. It's brilliant tactical thinking. It's decisive action. It's not passive behavior, taking whatever the adults give you; it's making your own destiny and solving your own problems.

Now let us return to Oliver, after his unfortunate soup incident. Eventually, Oliver is taken in by a mortician. And guess what? Spank spank! Abuse abuse! And then it's on to the streets of London, where he meets the Artful Dodger, Fagin, and the dastardly Bill Sikes. Good grief, can't the kid get a break?

Well, no, he can't. Because, you see, he's not driving the bus, he's riding in it. He's not guiding the story, he's bouncing around it like a pinball. He's the puppet with no control of his strings.

It seems to be a running theme throughout Dickens' work. Tiny Tim, David Copperfield, Pip of *Great Expectations*, Nell Trent of *The Old Curiosity Shop*. All rather powerless child characters whose skills rarely, if ever, exceed those of adults. Mythical heroes? Fuhgettaboutit.

Consider also Jim Hawkins of *Treasure Island*. Jim is no pushover, but it's the adults of the story who drive things and predominantly dictate the action. After all, Jim is just a child. What can a child do that an adult can't do better? Answer: nothing.

Oh, not true, you say. Jim Hawkins shows us that a child can do those noble, non-active things. A child can forgive. A child can be a friend. A child can let Long John Silver go in the end. And isn't that all that matters really?

Well, no, it isn't. It's important, yes. It's part of what makes our modern child heroes so likeable and valiant. But these days, it's not enough. Can you imagine a Harry Potter in which Harry runs to Dumbledore or Professor McGonagall whenever something is afoot and then follows them around while they solve the problem for him? What an exciting romp that would be. We could call it *Harry Potter and the Adults Who Save the Sorcerer's Stone*.

Pardon me while I stifle a yawn.

But what about Huck Finn? you ask. *Or Tom Sawyer. Aren't they heroes? Don't they drive the story?* And I'd say, *yes of course.* Absolutely. But what can Tom or Huck do that an adult can't do better? And what are the stakes? Tom wants someone to whitewash the fence. And Huck wants to escape his drunkard abusive father (again, the victim) and help Jim escape from slavery. Tom and Huck are heroes, no question, but much like Encyclopedia Brown, their reach is limited and their potential is low. They're ragamuffins. Scoundrels. Uneducated troublemakers with bucketloads of charm. We love them for it, sure. We adore them, yes. We acknowledge their literary merit, absolutely. But neither Tom nor Huck is a child hero in the post–*Ender's Game* sense.

This isn't to say that *Ender's Game* is better than *Adventures of Huckleberry Finn* or that Mark Twain's work would be rejected if it were submitted for publication today. I'm merely pointing out the shift in our perception of the child hero.

With *Ender's Game*, children were suddenly empowered. Adults still have all the authority, but the child heroes aren't letting that stop them. They're hopping into the driver's seat and pushing the accelerator to the floor. So what if they have to sit on a few phonebooks or tie a block of wood to the gas pedal to reach it? They're driving, baby.

Granted, not all children in fiction these days are out there defeating Voldemort or fighting the Greek gods; small-scale heroes are as prevalent as always. And you could argue that *Ender's Game* wasn't the first to feature a mythic child hero. (The Chronicles of Narnia spring to mind.) But even in the instances that pre-date *Ender's Game*, I'd argue that no child hero better demonstrated the character traits and story structure of the true mythic hero.

The Divine Child

We've discussed how Ender Wiggin is a mythic hero, but he also fits another archetype as well, that of the divine child. It was psychologist Carl Jung who first introduced the idea of the divine child, which manifests itself as a child god or a young hero. The divine child is a symbol of hope and a new beginning. He or she normally comes into the world by way of a miraculous birth, and often possesses a unique understanding of the world that grants special insight or power. The story of the Christ Child is a good example. Young Anakin Skywalker is another. Both are virgin births, both possess special abilities, and both bring new hope and promise to their universes. Another example is Jake Chambers from Stephen King's The Dark Tower series. Jake is a boy who miraculously enters the world and who possesses supernatural abilities, wisdom, and heroic attributes that help bring order and hope to Mid-World.

Ender Wiggin fits the bill as well. Consider Ender's birth. He's a Third, a statistical oddity. The population laws are explicit and stringently enforced. Yet because of the potential for greatness within the Wiggin home, the International Fleet gives its blessing and allows Ender to be born. He is, in that sense, a miracle. By the rules of the universe, he should not exist. And yet he does. That alone endows Ender with an aura of uniqueness. From the moment he leaves the womb, he's special.

In his book *The Archetypes and the Collective Unconscious*, Jung says that following this miraculous birth, the divine child can further be identified by four characteristics.

1. The abandonment of the child

Moses was set adrift on the Nile River. Paris was left abandoned on the mountainside. But Ender wasn't abandoned, was he? After all, he *chose* to leave his family and go to Battle School. Well, yes, that's true, but once he gets there, the International Fleet orchestrates his abandonment and blocks all contact from those he loves. He gets no messages from Valentine, no loving hugs from his mother, no words of encouragement from his father, and Graff works overtime to isolate Ender and keep him detached from other students. "His isolation can't be broken," says Graff. "He can never come to believe that anybody will help him out, *ever*."

2. The invincibility of the child

In most myths, this is a magical attribute. Immortality. Super-human strength. Bulletproof skin. In Ender's case, invincibility isn't the product of a magic elixir or divine parentage; it comes from the power of Ender's mind. He's invincible because he's smarter than every enemy he faces.

It's interesting, really. Ender's story is a trail of battles in which the odds are stacked against him, with each battle being more fierce and more impossible than the one before. Yet never once does Ender fail. Not against Stilson. Not in the Battle Room. Not against Bonzo. Not against the for-mics. Even when Ender is wet and alone and defenseless and outnumbered a thousand to one, he never goes down.

3. The hermaphroditism of the child

Did I just use a variant of the word *hermaphrodite*? Why, yes, yes I did. We have Mr. Carl Jung to thank for that.

And though it may strike you as strange, we can place a check in this box for Ender as well. Ender is a psychological hermaphrodite. He is the marriage of Valentine and Peter. Valentine is the archetypal female, demonstrating compassion and love and empathy, whereas Peter is the archetypal male, exuding violence and anger and dominance. Throw those two archetypes into the archetype blender and out comes Ender Wiggin.

Valentine would argue this point, and does so in the novel. She screams at Graff, "Ender is not like Peter! He is not like Peter in any way!" But that's not entirely true. In some ways, Ender is like Peter. They're both strategically brilliant, and they both strike when the situation requires it. It's for this reason that Ender worries throughout the novel that he is slowly becoming like his brother. "I am just like Peter. Take my monitor away, and I am just like Peter."

And yet because of the qualities Ender inherits from Valentine, he is not Peter. Her compassion counters Peter's selfishness. Her calm counters Peter's rage. So Ender has all of Peter's greatness but none of Peter's baggage. And he has all of Valentine's heart and none of her trepidation. He is everything great that the Wiggin family can offer—all of the good and none of the evil—rolled up into a single human being.

In fact, Ender exists for this very reason. The International Fleet wanted the best of Peter and Valentine, and so they rolled the dice and allowed John Paul and Theresa to conceive a third child. Fortunately for everyone, that bet paid off.

4. The child as beginning and end

The divine child is the beginning and end of life. The Christ Child is the beginning of Christ's higher law and the end of the mosaic law. Young Anakin Skywalker is the beginning of the rise of the Sith Lords while at the same time promising to be the one who ends the Siths' rule and "brings balance to the Force" by killing the Emperor.

Ender clearly fits this aspect of the divine child as well. He is the end of life because he annihilates the formics. And he is the beginning of life because he discovers the cocoon and with it the promise of a formic rebirth. He is, therefore, both sides of the coin. Death and life. Despair and hope. The tomb and the womb. Killer and savior.

The Personhood of Children

So yes, *Ender's Game* fits the hero-myth formula, and yes, it's filled with Jungian archetypes, but as anyone who has read the novel will tell you, Ender's story is anything but formulaic. Formulas don't move us. Formulas don't make us cry one moment and cheer the next. Formulas don't have soul. And *Ender's Game* is dripping with soul.

That soul of course is the soul of Ender Wiggin, the short Clint Eastwood, the modern child hero, the boy who showed us how significant a child's contribution can be.

And in the end, isn't that the point of *Ender's Game*? Card didn't set out to create a child character who sounds and acts like an adult. He set out to create a true depiction of a child. Ender is who he is because Card genuinely believes in the capacity of children to think great things and achieve great things. It's a belief Card has held all his life.

> Never in my entire childhood did I feel like a child. I felt like a person all along—the same person I am today. I never felt that I spoke childishly. I never felt that my emotions and desires were somehow less real than adult emotions and desires. And in writing *Ender's Game*, I forced the audience to experience the lives of these children from that perspective—the perspective in which their feelings and decisions are just as real and important as any adults. (*Ender's Game*, Introduction, 1991)

Well, if that was Card's intent, then he can give himself a gold star because that's exactly what *Ender's Game* does. It "asserts the personhood of children" (*Ender's Game*, Introduction). It validates them. It challenges the belief that they are the weaker of the two classes. It opens the floodgates of child-hero stories, the effect of which we are still seeing today and will likely see for a long time to come.

But most important, *Ender's Game* gives us Ender Wiggin, who, to those of us who discovered him in our youth, is more than a character on a page or even a kindred spirit. Ender is an epiphany. He is the realization that maybe, just maybe, we can do great things too.

Back in the desert ghost town, two figures stand facing each other across a wide stretch of dirt in the middle of the street. One is tall and lean and dusty, with one corner of his poncho folded back to give him easy access to his gun. The other figure is much shorter. A boy. His flashsuit is tight but unfrozen, his helmet secure. The tip of his weapon is already bright with a dot of light. They stare each other down, neither flinching. A shrill music breaks the silence. *Whaa-whaa-whaa.* There are whispers that these two are evenly matched, that neither of them will come out alive.

I disagree.

My money's on the boy.

Aaron Johnston is a New York Times *bestselling author. He and Orson Scott Card wrote* Earth Unaware, *which is the first of a series of prequel novels to* Ender's Game. *The second novel,* Earth Afire, *will be released by TOR in summer 2013. Aaron also adapted Orson Scott Card's* Ender in Exile *and* Speaker for the Dead *for Marvel Comics. Other comics credits within the Ender universe include* League War, Mazer in Prison, *and* Formic Wars. *He and Orson Scott Card are also the co-authors of the novel* Invasive Procedures. *Follow him at aaronwjohnston.com or on Twitter @AaronWJohnston.*

A TEENLESS WORLD

METTE IVIE HARRISON

I was at a bar following a SFF convention a few years ago, chatting up an editor I had hoped to interest in a new adult fantasy novel of mine. The conversation turned to my previously published YA novels, among them *The Princess and the Hound*. The adult genre editor, not surprisingly, had never heard of the title. I mentioned that it had been given a good review by Orson Scott Card, and the editor's interest seemed to perk up. But it wasn't my book he was interested in. Instead, he asked me point blank, "Why is Orson Scott Card so interested in torturing children?" *Ender's Game* was at the top of his list of proofs for his assertion. I goggled at him, but he wouldn't let it go as a rhetorical question. He wanted me to defend child torture in *Ender's Game*, it seemed.

I tried to say that, as far as I knew, Orson Scott Card was not a sadist or a child-hater. His books showed characters who faced difficult things, and it seemed to me that one of the reasons many readers fell in love with his books was that he didn't take it easy on younger characters, whether children or teenagers. Because life doesn't take it easy on the young, and books that coddle them in the way that parents sometimes seem to want may be comforting, but they are not the books that seem real and lead readers to feel intimately attached to them. In short, *Ender's Game* is a book that younger readers read precisely because it treats them and the characters their age as people, no different really than adults. And that is something teens in particular desperately crave, to be seen not as children who need to be sheltered but as people who are capable of determining their own futures, for good or ill.

The very idea of *teenager* is a modern concept developed in the twentieth century as part of the fight for child labor laws and the development of the federal school system. (The first appearance of the word *teenage* is in the *Reader's Digest* in 1941, but it appears to have been in common use by then.) It was originally coined as a way of describing those who were fully grown physically and had been considered ready for adult jobs in earlier centuries, but to whom the government now extended its protection because it no longer considered them to be adults.

What is the age of adulthood? One might argue that it is the age at which military service is allowed, which would be only seventeen. Or that it is the age at which teens are legally allowed to drop out of high school and begin full-time work. This age has recently been changed to eighteen from sixteen in about half the states, in order to encourage teens to stay in school. Driver's license privileges are also part of our traditional definition of adulthood. They begin in many states at fifteen or sixteen, but full privileges are withheld until eighteen or even later. Other adult privileges are also withheld until a certain age. Tobacco use is allowed by most states at age eighteen (nineteen in Utah and a handful of others). Voting privileges begin at age eighteen. But the very fact that we have different state laws on many of these passages to adulthood would suggest that there is a great deal of debate on what it means. If we say eighteen is the age of adulthood, it is certainly provisional. For instance, we have extended the age of drinking to twenty-one in most states, which implies that we still consider those between eighteen and twenty-one too juvenile to make their own choices about alcohol use.

I think it might be more useful to define adulthood as the age at which many children stop being financially dependent on or living with parents or guardians. By this reasoning, many children are pushing back full adulthood until well into their twenties. In fact, the new health care laws seem to imply that before age twenty-six, most people are still children and should expect parental support financially. The idea that parents are expected to pay for a college education, and that until this is finished a parent's job is not, also extends the teen years far later than they once were. Even in publishing, the term *young adult* has begun to include the college years, when at one time in the past, it was assumed that adulthood had already been achieved. Why are we as a society postponing the years of adulthood? Is it because we are only now getting scientific proof about when the development of the brain reaches its zenith? I don't think so.

My belief is that this is about technology, the changes that technology has made to our world, and the length of time it takes to learn the skills necessary to contribute to a technologically advanced world. Yes, many children seem more adept on computers, cell phones, and other technologies than adults are. Many children are learning to read at a younger age than the previous generation and doing more complex math by the end of high school. Nonetheless, a high school graduate cannot expect to earn a decent living. Earnings from a full-time minimum wage job are no longer sufficient for raising a family. Even an undergraduate degree may not be enough to be truly competitive in the world of future technological advancements. So it makes sense to give children more time in which to develop the skills they need to become adults, to extend those years during which children look like adults but are not expected to work as adults do.

But with this extension of childhood comes an extension of parental guidance, of teenage rebellion and disdain for adults who stifle real talent and creativity in their attempt to protect. *Ender's Game* shows us a different world, in which those who might in our world be called children or teenagers and be allowed time to develop are instead recruited to fight a war. In fact, *child*, *teenage*, and *adult* are not useful categories in a world on the edge of destruction, only *effective* and *ineffective*. Because of the exigent circumstances of the war against the formics, as soon as children are capable of acting in adult ways, they are allowed—in fact required—to be placed in adult roles. This is the sheerest meritocracy that is imaginable, free of age-based biases. And it isn't a horror story to teens. It is the kind of world teens go back to read about again and again, and if they are frightened by it, they also seem empowered, far more than the adults who watch teens reading *Ender's Game* are sometimes comfortable with. They seem to want teens to be disgusted, to confirm the adults' ideas that the world of *Ender's Game* is too grown up for teens to relate to. But that is far from the truth.

Ender's Game begins when Ender is six years old and the climax of the book is when he is only ten years old. The first thing we as readers hear from Ender is his thoughts when an adult tells him that his monitor coming off "won't hurt a bit." He thinks, "It was a lie, of course, that it wouldn't hurt a bit. But since adults always said it when it was going to hurt, he could count on that as an accurate prediction of the future. Sometimes lies were more dependable than the truth." The complaint that adults are hypocrites, that they say one thing and do something completely different, that they declare a set of morality rules for children but break those rules themselves again and again, is common among teens in our world. Ender's understanding of this at the age of six certainly shows his precocity.

Ender does not think of himself as a teenager, of course. Nor does the text ever suggest that he has the other attributes we normally associate with teenagers. He is not whiny, abrasive, rude to parents or other adults. He does not demand responsibility that he does not deserve. He doesn't show irresponsible behavior or talk back. Ender has the thinking capacity of an adult, and he treats adults as equals, criticizing them when he sees that they are wrong. He has the tone of a soldier who tells a superior officer precisely what is wrong with the system. You can compare his complaints to Graff with those of David Weber's Honor Harrington or Lois McMaster Bujold's Aral Vorkosigan—adult characters in popular military science fiction worlds. And this is precisely what is appealing about *Ender's Game* to teens, in my view. They are imagining a future in which they might be valued and judged as adults are, based on their merits and usefulness to society, and not dismissed out of hand because of their age. *Ender's Game* is not at all disturbing to teens. Ender has what teens want, which is the adult world given to them, fully, right now.

When Ender first enters Battle School, he is told, "You won't have a normal childhood." In fact, what they mean is that his childhood, such as it has been, is over. He won't have any childhood at all. He is now an adult, entering the army. The conversations between Ender and the other boys in Battle School aren't childlike at all. Ender demands to be called *sir* and he calls his team *gentlemen*. The laughing and jokes here are actually more adult than childlike, despite the occasional references to farting. Rat Army commander Rose the Nose tells newly conscripted Ender, "You ain't nothing but a pinheaded prick of a goy," and then there follows a long discussion of what *goy* means, on an adult level. Rose tells Ender that Dink Meeker is God. Ender asks Rose who Rose is and is given the answer "the personnel officer who hired God." Later, when the other, older boys are trying to intimidate Ender, Alai asks him, "They scare you, too? They slap you up in the bathroom? Stick you head in the pissah? Somebody gots a gun up you bung?" Pretty strong stuff.

In fact, this is the kind of language that my editor in YA would steer me clear of. I've been asked not to use the word *piss*, let alone suggest sodomy. The parents who patrol the internet for their children of all ages and who post reviews for "clean books" as if that is a shiny sticker of approval would never accept language like this in a YA novel. I suspect it would be difficult to avoid parental complaints when teaching *Ender's Game* in a high school—unless perhaps the parents have read the book themselves and felt how powerfully it speaks to teens. The strong language and content is part of the reason that the book continues to have more success published as an adult book rather than a teen book, though the protagonist is the traditional age of a middle grade novel's, even younger than a YA novel's protagonist. (The label and the shelf placement in bookstores and libraries hasn't stopped kids of differing ages from picking up and loving *Ender's Game*, though. Nor from feeling as though this is the book that first spoke to them, that first invited them into the adult world. It is the book that they remember as one of the finest novels of science fiction ever.)

Card's genius is that he puts such harsh, adult words in the mouths of children and makes them believable. Not just because these kids are super-smart, though they are. The dialogue is believable because these kids are filling the adult roles that make their words necessary. And these kids are capable of filling these roles precisely because they are allowed to be, forced to be. Teens who read *Ender's Game* love it because they can imagine themselves to be Ender or Petra or Bean. They can imagine that adults take them seriously, too.

The null grav suit that all the children of Battle School put on can be read as a symbolic costume of adulthood. They need to wear it in order to become soldiers in space, but it isn't all fun and games. Ender says null gravity is "frightening, disorienting." The suits are confining: "It was harder to make precise movements, since the suits bent just a bit slower, resisted a bit more than any clothing they had ever worn before." For children becoming adults too soon, the expectations of adulthood would feel this way. But Ender figures out immediately the right way to see the world with a suit on. He moves past the feeling of discomfort and finds out that, with this adult suit on, value systems change. *Down* and *up* become malleable concepts and require him, as a real adult, to see the world in its full-color complexity.

In this context, in which the survival of the human race depends on its soldiers' ability to not just see this complexity but also use it to take advantage of the ever-changing battleground of space, Ender's age is actually an asset because it makes him more flexible. But in our world, many children have this flexibility and are not praised for it. To the contrary, when they express their new vision of the world, they are often beaten down, told to show respect to authority, to the way things have always been. Sometimes they give up and simply follow the rules instead of reinventing them, pretending that this is accepting adulthood. Ender, in the book, is in a unique and enviable position because the adults around him are desperate enough that they actually listen to his crazy ideas and let him see what happens when he relies on them. Teens in our world are rarely given this chance.

Still, Ender does face adult censure at times. He just deals with it in a way that isn't very teen. He doesn't rebel. He simply ignores it and does what he wants anyway. For instance, when the adults who are behind the scenes of Battle School decide to start making it impossible for Ender and his toon to win and changing the rules of the battles the children play, Ender could react with anger and depression as Dink does. "It's the teachers. They're the enemy," says Dink. They've tried to promote him, but he refuses and keeps going back to his place in his toon. Dink continues:

> They get us to fight each other, to hate each other. The game is everything. Win win win. It amounts to nothing. We kill ourselves, go crazy trying to beat each other and all the time the old bastards are watching us, studying us, discovering our weak points, deciding whether we're good enough or not. Well, good enough for what?

Here at last we have typical teenage rebelliousness, but notice that Ender rejects it. He has no interest in being a teenager, in being helpless and complaining about adults manipulating him. In fact, Ender's careful use of the mind game makes the reader begin to wonder who is manipulating whom. Are the adults doing the manipulating or is Ender? I think teen readers may be subtly shown that Dink's way is easier, but Ender's way is the way to really be successful. To refuse to rebel but to find a way to make the game of adulthood your own—that is the way to find power in the adult world, and that is what teens ultimately want.

That teens are as capable as adults when it comes to understanding the world, and more capable of changing it, is reinforced when we hear what Peter and Valentine are doing on Earth while Ender is at Battle School. They are two years older than Ender, which makes them eight and ten when he starts Battle School and twelve and fourteen when he defeats the formics—classic teen years. And yet what do Peter and Valentine do that is teenlike? They talk about troop movements in Russia, about world politics, things that teens are supposed to be completely uninterested in. "They call us children and treat us like mice," says Valentine of the adults around them. This is a fairly typical teenage complaint, but Valentine and Peter take it to the next logical step and begin to write essays on two sides of the political spectrum in an attempt to remake the world.

With the internet (which Scott imagined clearly years before it was widely used) children are able to act like adults. No one knows their age, and so they can become whatever it is that their ideas and abilities mean they can become. Peter says, "We don't have to wait until we're grown up and safely put away in some career," a line that could easily be put in the mouth of a bratty teenager and dismissed. But Card doesn't dismiss it. He never dismisses Valentine and Peter's grand schemes. Instead, he shows them coming about exactly as a teen might imagine it happening. They want to be adults, they find a way to be seen as adults, and they are perfectly capable of being adults. They move directly from childhood to adulthood without any stage in between. They don't need coddling. They don't need the guidance of adults. They don't need college or an internship or a few years still at home with Mom and Dad helping them pay back student loans and get a car paid off. This makes one wonder who the long extension of teenage-hood in our modern times is really serving. Is it really for the sake of the children, who need the help of the adults? Or is it the adults who need to be needed, need to live in a world in which they have the most power, in which a child's years are extended and extended again to keep any power out of their reach?

"Ender Wiggin must believe that no matter what happens, no adult will ever, ever step in to help him in any way. He must believe that to the core of his soul, that he can only do what he and the other children work out for themselves. If he does not believe that, then he will never reach the peak of his abilities," says Graff. This push off the cliff into adulthood is precisely what adults in our world now think they are saving teens from. They keep giving them safety nets, but the truth that *Ender's Game* seems to argue is that teens will never reach the peak of their abilities until the safety nets are taken away and children are allowed to design their own wings in ways adults have never thought possible before, as Ender reinvents the null grav suit. He uses the same materials, but it becomes something utterly different in his hands. What are we adults who hold back adulthood from our children depriving the world of? What inventions are we shrugging our shoulders at, patting the heads of children and telling them that when they are "safely put away in a career," they will be able to try something moderately innovative, so long as it is innovative in the same ways that other successful inventors have been innovative?

When the formics are defeated, Ender and the other children finally find out the truth about this battle, that it has been real, that they have truly killed the enemy. Petra and Bean and Ender laugh rather grimly at the thought of going back to being kids, to a regular middle school on Earth. But what else can be done with them? There is a trial to decide how to punish the adult Graff for misdeeds during the war, and some of the other children who are lesser figures in the victory against the formics are welcomed back. But no one knows what to do with Ender. He is *persona non grata*, not because he is responsible for xenocide (that judgment comes later), but because he is a child who is not a child, and although he was useful during the war, he cannot fit into normal society anymore. In the end, this is the real tragedy for teen readers who want to believe that they will be accepted as adults. Even in Ender's world, it's only a one-time, special-circumstances kind of situation. It doesn't mean that society has changed. The attractive futuristic world of *Ender's Game* for teens is over, even before the book itself is, and the jolt back into reality hurts.

After winning the war, what Ender hates the most is the cheers of the colonists when they see him. He thinks, "*They* didn't blame him for any of his murders because it wasn't his fault he was just a *child*." But Ender knows he wasn't a child, and he has no excuses for what he has done. He'd rather be court-martialed himself than watch Graff be court-martialed in his place. He wants to be treated as an adult, but even in *Ender in Exile*, when he has gone through puberty, when he is being sent to run a whole colony, he is still treated as a teen (not as a child but still a step back from his previous position), as incapable of taking on an adult role as yet. He has to prove himself again and again.

I am interested in this topic because of my own experience as a teen—when I felt as if the main role of adults was to hold me back from adulthood under the guise of protecting me—because I write for teens, and because I am a parent of four teens now. I am often surprised at those around me who roll their eyes at their teens' complaints, who sigh with fond memories of their children's early years, and who seem to disdain everything teenage. They wonder how it is that I can enjoy my teens' company during these years. But simply giving my teens the ability to make their own choices in their lives has made them very unteenly. They don't make extravagant gestures of rebellion because there is very little for them to rebel against. When my teen can't do a family job because she is busy doing homework or being in a play at school, I don't make a fuss about it. When a teen needs some time off to spend with friends, I encourage it as I would encourage a healthy adult friend to take care of her emotional needs. When my teen decides that playing an instrument is taking up valuable time that might be spent pursuing another aspect of her life that will help her in her career, I don't try to talk her out it. I commend her for the adult decision she has made. My main interest as a parent is in helping my nearly adult children get what they want in life once they have figured out what that is. I am not interested in making them do things I think they should want to do. I expect my teens to give me respect, but I also offer them respect for their areas of expertise in turn. I am flexible about rules of the house in much the same way that I would be with another adult who lived in my home.

In the world of children's literature, *young adult* and not *teen* is the term that has been used to describe literature written for those over the age of twelve, and this is the age group that has seen the greatest increase in book buying in the last twenty years. From a handful of books available in the children's section of the bookstore in the seventies, YA has become a publishing juggernaut. Certainly Stephenie Meyer's Twilight series, which for at least one year recently accounted for four out of every five books purchased in America, should be given some credit for this. And then there is J.K. Rowling's Harry Potter, which created a huge reading public of children eager for new books. But the truth of the matter is that, if not for the adults buying these YA and other children's titles, there would not be the same publishing phenomenon. Adults are reading YA in huge numbers. Why? Because YA books are shorter and easier to read and Americans don't have the attention span for more adult books? I think it is more likely because, as Garth Nix argued recently, YA books are merely a subset of adult books, as young adults themselves are a subset of adults.

The latest trend in YA is so-called *dystopian novels*, including Suzanne Collins' wonderful *The Hunger Games*, James Dashner's *The Maze Runner*, and Ally Condie's *Matched*. But are they really dystopian in the way that adult dystopian novels have been grim depictions of a future that cannot be changed? I don't think so. These books show teens in charge of revolutions against corrupt governments that adults have done nothing to fight. They are books that show teens with adult power.

In a way, *Ender's Game* is a forerunner for this kind of book because of both the difficult circumstances in which Ender and the other children of Battle School are placed, and the dark future world the book depicts, where humanity is at risk and there are dangerous enemies never before faced. In such books, as in *Ender's Game*, teens' decisions have life-and-death consequences, and there are no adults to protect them. Teens learn what they need to learn about survival in the adult world. They make hard choices and sometimes lose friends for the sake of principles. They give up childhood willingly because they want the power that they can only get with adulthood. It's no wonder that *Ender's Game* is still being read. Even as YA explodes, teens are still treated as Ender was when he had done what adults needed him to do and they didn't know what to do with him: when he became a *teen*, the uncategorizable, the unnecessary, the not-yet and still-to-be.

Mette Ivie Harrison *is the author of* Mira, Mirror, *the Princess and the Hound series,* Tris and Izzie, *and the forthcoming* The Rose Throne *(May 2013). She is a competitive triathlete and has a PhD in Germanic Languages and Literatures from Princeton University (1995). She has five children and lives in Layton, Utah. Her website is www.metteivieharrison.com.*

Q. What experiences did you draw from to create Ender and Bean? Your representation of the "gifted child" demographic is spot-on. My heart is closer to those two characters than Holden Caulfield, which is quite odd for an adolescent fighting the clutches of cynicism and role confusion.

A. Let me deal first with the matter of adolescence and Holden Caulfield:

When I finally got around to reading *Catcher in the Rye* I was already in my forties. I found Holden Caulfield to be a believable "bright adolescent"—self-centered, shallow, arrogant, and nowhere near as bright as he thinks he is.

But Salinger chose Holden Caulfield because he wanted to write about just such a shallow, arrogant character; I chose Ender and Bean for very different reasons, and so they were very different children. For one thing, they really *were* smarter than everyone around them, rather than merely thinking they were.

More important was the fact that Ender Wiggin was *not* an adolescent in *Ender's Game*. He was still a child, and was held by Battle School in a prolonged childhood, where his entire reality was created by the adults around him. Where he was able to break out of that reality was only in ways that were useful to the purposes of the adults; his adolescence did not come until after the war.

In fact, his adolescence consisted of all his years as an iconoclastic speaker for the dead, a role that is as isolated and skeptical as that of any adolescent, but one that was ultimately generous in a way that is utterly beyond a Holden Caulfield. That is, Ender Wiggin remained true to his inner magnanimity even during his time of self-invention and questioning. *Speaker for the Dead* takes up his story at the end of his adolescence, when he is ready to commit to membership in a community and to take a permanent adult role.

Thus the story of Ender Wiggin completely skips over the very phase of life that *Catcher in the Rye* is devoted to.

Bean, however, is forced into a premature adolescence by the struggle for survival in the hideous version of Rotterdam I invented for *Ender's Shadow*. He is cynical; he questions everything, trusts no one, and thinks only of himself. This makes him very much more like Holden Caulfield—only, again, much smarter, and with far more important things at stake than are ever involved in the shallow life of Holden Caulfield.

It takes Bean a while to see past his own survival issues and recognize his responsibility to the human race as a whole— a species to which he does not feel himself to belong. But that very feeling of not-belonging *is* adolescence, and his decision to act for the sake of humanity is also a decision to become an adult. It is in that adult role that he functions thereafter, even to the point of embracing marriage and childrearing as the primary objective of the rest of his life. It was a commitment he thought would be impossible to him; yet he made that commitment, as most adolescents do, when they finally decide to grow up.

As to Ender and Bean serving as an accurate depiction of gifted children: I'm on very firm ground here. Though I was no world-changing genius as a child, I was very bright, with all the social burdens that imposes. I was fortunate to be in the California school system back when it was committed to ability-grouping and bringing all students to achieve their maximum potential, rather than miseducating everyone in the name of political correctness, as the California schools are committed to doing today.

The result was that I met other bright kids, and saw the problems and the benefits of unusually high intelligence. I knew how bright kids talk to each other, and how they learn to camouflage themselves in order to get along. I am amused by adults who say, "I've worked with gifted kids, and they don't talk like the kids in *Ender's Game*." To them my answer is, "They don't talk like that *to you*."

The fact is that I modeled Ender's verbal ability on my son Geoffrey, who was *five* years old at the time I wrote about Ender as a six-year-old. Anyone who knew Geoffrey at that age has no problem believing the dialogue of the children in Battle School.

It is also worth remembering that military command is impossible without the ability to formulate plans and present them clearly and persuasively to superiors and subordinates. So part of what was tested for in admitting children to Battle School was verbal effectiveness.

Here is the great secret, however: *All children are able to identify with the Battle School kids, regardless of their level of academic talent, because *all* children feel themselves to be autonomous individuals, with clear motives and moral reasoning. They are "childish" only in their inexperience and ignorance; if you give them experience and education, their brains are capable of all the *thought* that adults are capable of. And, prior to the onslaught of adolescent hormones, they are sometimes capable of making decisions not less but *more* rationally than adults.

So my creation of all these bright children comes from my memory of being one and my close observation of children since then, whether labeled as geniuses or not. Brilliant children are not so different from non-brilliant ones as outsiders often suppose. The skills we label as "intelligence" are not dissimilar to the skills we label as "athletic" or "musical" or "social." Children are good at different things, but at core they are people, and a writer who thinks otherwise will write them very badly.

—*OSC*

Q. A trivial question, but it's always bothered me: From the short story to the novel, why did you change Ender's surname from Wiggins to Wiggin?

A. Oh, it's worse than you think. I changed from *Wiggins* to *Wiggin within* the short story. So when I came to write the novel, I basically flipped a coin and chose *Wiggin.*

I have a terrible memory for names. I have to keep a table of all the names in an ongoing book, and then I consult it frequently, because otherwise I'll misremember a character's name and change back and forth throughout. Even *with* such a table, the character *Olivenko* in *Pathfinder* spent much of the book as *Ovilenko*, and I no longer remember which was the original choice.

—*OSC*

ENDER ON LEADERSHIP

COLONEL TOM RUBY
(USAF, RETIRED)

I was a relative latecomer to *Ender's Game*. It's not that I didn't know about the book. It's not even that I hadn't had it recommended to me. Only a bunch of times by people I trusted. I remember visiting my old Air Force Academy mentor, Colonel Jim Heald, and his family in Florida when I was attending Squadron Officer School in Alabama in 1993. Jim's oldest son, Mike, was telling me that I really needed to read this book. I said, "Okay," and never did. I think I finally went to *Ender's Game* when I was mature enough to read the books that people I trusted recommended to me, regardless of genre or what phase of life I was in. And bully for me. All I'd done by delaying was deny myself eight years of good thinking. But it was more than good thinking I denied myself. Had I read the book earlier in my career, I could have benefitted from Ender's experiences by applying them to my own as a rising Air Force officer, one who endured and battled through much of the head-scratchingly unbelievable bureaucratic mess that nattered Ender.

When I finally did read *Ender's Game*, I was a major in the Air Force with a line number to lieutenant colonel, waiting for the day of my promotion to roll around. I was also a doctoral student at the University of Kentucky, studying political science and focusing on morality in warfare. Living in the university environment rather than on or near a base, it was most interesting for me to see how similar some of the sociological issues of the university were to those of the Air Force.

I was also interested in how un-bridgeable a chasm it was. The two societies (one academic and the other martial), despite their tremendous natural commonalities, didn't know anything about each other, and were too leery of each other to want to find common ground. But inside each was an organizational model that you could have stepped right into without knowing anything other than what you learned from *Ender's Game*. Although they ought to be natural allies, the Academy and the military often fight each other as if they were mortal enemies. But within each world there are also parallel battles—battles for ideological supremacy and battles for leadership over those they ostensibly lead. When I read *Ender's Game* I was stunned at how precisely the book painted both worlds I was in at the time. I was stunned as well at what I had been missing all those years in not reading the book. And after earning my degree, I soon learned firsthand even more about those ideological battles, not *in* the book, but *through* it.

By the time I was senior enough to influence an organization, I was a senior faculty member at the Air Force's Air Command and Staff College, a premier graduate school where the top tier of Air Force majors attend a yearlong resident program of graduate study in international relations, history, and strategic studies. While there, I made reading *Ender's Game* a mandatory part of the curriculum. I then experienced some of the same issues, such as resistance to longstanding paradigms, that Ender slogged through during his service.

Many of my colleagues, civilian and military, historian and political scientist, questioned my inclusion of *Ender's Game* in the curriculum at the Staff College. *What can we learn*, some vociferously and indignantly asked, *from a science fiction book about something that will never happen?* Some had never been challenged to defend their core beliefs about how we know what we know. Others hadn't yet learned to trust their colleagues' recommendations about something as important as their time. Most didn't understand that the only place in which they could explore the sociology of a situation that has not yet happened is in fiction. And they certainly didn't know that science fiction is not about robots and alien invasions and long space journeys. Those things are only vehicles for exploring social situations and human nature, for thought games in which they could ask, *How would people interact if this happened?* or, *Would the societal structure stand up to this stress?*

I think the lessons military leaders can learn from *Ender's Game* are numerous and simple. And that nearly guarantees that most won't bother trying. It is ironic that

Ender is perhaps best known by a segment of society that will never serve in uniform: those sci-fi fans who understand that the genre is about sociology and thinking about what might happen. (That same hypothetical elegance is what has made *Ender's Game* so appealing to Hollywood. But could any screenwriter truly present Ender as he is without neutering him into something a producer thinks that a kid ought to be? If ignoring Ender is bad, then rendering him hapless, lucky, or a puppet is a crime against his [fictional] being.)

So for both military leaders that seek to better themselves and for civilians unsure of how realistic the story is, let us consider some military leadership truths of *Ender's Game*. Ender was no dupe. He didn't just ride a wave of subordinate success. He was not the accidental hero. Ender was for real. Just like so many military leaders throughout history and living today are for real. We'll consider Ender's leadership strengths and then explore the battle he was forced to fight against his own leadership while preparing to fight the formics.

Ender learned very early on that skill and excellence are at once both one's means to promotion and a threat to peers and immediate superiors. So it is in the military today and so it has been in the military throughout history. One must perform well in order to be recognized. But such performance also marks a stud performer for retribution. Ender is the youngest kid ever in Battle School (at least until Bean comes along). When placed in his first army, he does exactly what his idiot boss tells him to do, and when it backfires on the idiot boss, the boss takes his anger out on Ender instead of either praising the kid for following directions or keeping his mouth shut and pondering the lesson from the Battle Room. The toon leaders Ender encounters when he first arrives at Battle School were all pretty much equally mediocre to average, and that's fine with them. It's more important not to rock the boat and be one of the guys than to try to excel and get ahead of one's peers.

The students knew that humanity had survived two attacks by the formics and that a third attack was imminent. But it is a sad reality of our human nature that so many will keep doing the same old thing day after day, even when failure is imminent or some catastrophic danger is looming. That truth applies to current as well as past militaries. In Baghdad during the autumn of 2004, I remember being stunned by the number of senior military leaders who said that all we needed to do to "win the war" was *more, better, longer*. More forces. Better execution of (unarguably bad) plans. Staying there longer. Just like the toon leaders Ender encounters upon reaching Battle School. Ender, on the other hand, doesn't accept the status quo, because it means only one thing: certain annihilation.

Ender accepts the situation as it is and not as he wishes it would be. He does the same when it comes to his soldiers. He knows he doesn't have the best subordinate talent. He realizes that the leaders at Battle School are giving him kids who are young and inexperienced, just like he was when he first arrived. Ender feels like every day they are stacking the deck against him, and they are. But he doesn't dwell on what he doesn't have.

He never complains about his army's lack of sleep, rest, or continuity; he learns from the moment he takes command that pandering to his people doesn't make them better. When he discusses the situation with the Battle School leadership and they explain to him that he's not training to fight older kids but the formics, he merely accepts the answer and gets back to training.

Ender consistently seeks out and finds whatever each other kid is able to contribute and makes use of that contribution toward achieving his army's goals. Furthermore, he always makes clear the significance of each person's contribution. Yet he never dwells on his own.

Ender is a deeply human character in the midst of a system designed specifically to eat away at his humanity and turn him into a tool. A thinking and learning tool, true, but a tool nonetheless. Ender fights to keep his humanity as much as he learns to defend humankind. His kiss of peace from Alai; his deep love for Valentine; his fear of becoming Peter; his deep resolve to fight back against the leadership and to preserve Christmas as a holiday—these are not mere literary tools of an overly humanistic author. Today, our military is filled with senior officers who truly believe that to show a human or, worse yet, a loving character is somehow weak and dangerous for the country they serve.

Consider the following words, which were actually sent in a directive to US forces from all services assigned to the Personnel Directorate staff in Afghanistan prior to Christmas 2011:

> Christmas Parties are an obstacle to productivity. 25 December is when we will get the most work done because everyone else is wasting energy on

things like trees and fat strangers in red suits. We at USFOR-A J1 will maximize this artificial lull in the battle to re-enforce our defensive positions and prepare to go on the offensive to close out the year. Clean weapons and efficient work processes will be all the gifts this year.

The saddest truth is not that this organization's leader sincerely meant what he wrote, but that this directive is indicative of countless others sent by military leaders around the world. Like Ender and his mates, military members find ways to slow down, give gifts, and reassert their humanity.

Part of being human is figuring out how to control what you can and know when you can't. Ender never assumed or acted as if he was a good leader or in complete control. He never ruled by fear and intimidation like other toon leaders (and so many generals in human history). Over the last twenty years, a disturbing trend has emerged that was once a joke but is now a sad reality. Whenever US Army officers gather in any room or formation, they immediately determine who has the most senior date of rank. It is the only way they know who is in charge, even when there is no need for anyone to be in charge. From that point on, younger officers grudgingly submit to the most senior person, even if they are the same rank. They eye him angrily and he plots how to annoy them all within the bounds of regulations and propriety. They call him a blockhead and all manner of other names, but they do what he says.

In Ender's case, he is incessantly put upon by students who are senior to him, regardless of how well he performs, simply because they are more senior. It is not until he has beaten every other army, and then multiple armies at one time with their own castoffs, that he earns respect and gains admiration from his more senior peers (but only some of them). Unlike those who intimidate their fellow trainees, Ender's actions earn him respect and neither he nor his subordinates ever doubt his command.

Ender knows he is far from perfect, yet he never dwells on that fact. Rather, he is the consummate lifelong learner. He is driven to get better. Not one minute of his day is wasted. He lies in bed at night reflecting on every encounter of the day, every action of every battle, every quirk of every fellow student. He reflects on his actions, and although he is hard on himself, he is truly objective and seeks his own betterment and that of his team. Ender studies other teams and their tactics, takes the good and incorporates those lessons into his own tactics, and even explains the mistakes to the vanquished . . . if they are smart enough to ask. He spends additional time practicing with Petra and realizes that, as brilliant as she is, her breaking point is lower than that of the other kids. He incessantly watches videos of previous formic battles and comes not only to learn their tactics but also to see how the videos were edited by the military to present a particular narrative and not the full reality. These two things, Ender's desire for betterment and his ability to accurately assess his performance (witness his self-reflection after his first command practice session), are his greatest leadership skills. Leading journals and researchers today cite the inability to assess one's own performance as the top flaw among senior leaders in all professions.

There comes a time for every person climbing the leadership ladder when he becomes aware that he is doing something right and thus is either being promoted or being groomed for promotion. That person has a choice to make: revel in his own perceived worthiness for promotion or realize that this promotion comes with new responsibility and new opportunity.

At first it is difficult for Ender to see the obligation that responsibility carries. He is getting berated every day by his commander. He is the youngest kid in any army. And when he is called in and told he has been promoted and given his own army, he is incredulous. He doesn't believe they would promote him early. All he can think about is how unprepared he is. Later, once he starts training his army and winning battles, it is readily apparent to him that he has a large measure of respect from everyone around him. But Ender never lets that go to his head.

Contrast Ender's attitude with that of leaders throughout history who let their successes turn into power trips and narcissistic self-aggrandizement. Picture the bombastic and often self-absorbed Patton and Montgomery, who often raced to parade in front of liberated towns first during World War II, and then contrast their inflated self-images with the humility of Washington, Lee, or Eisenhower. Ender falls in the latter category hands down. As a leader, he focuses on making his subordinates, peers, and superiors better instead of soaking in their adulation. While the other "boys" are laughing in the commanders' mess, Ender is in the Battle Room running nightly practice sessions above and beyond what the school requires.

I once had a close friend at an Air Force fighter wing who was crass, often on the verge of being in trouble, always under the watchful eye of the group commander, and often accused by some other pilots of putting himself above the squadron and wing. But the truth was far more subtle. You knew he never put himself first when the youngest and most inexperienced lieutenants all wanted to be on his wing during the toughest missions. He could devise the most complex strategy for a particular mission deep into heavily defended enemy territory, but if he thought that a single pilot in the entire force package couldn't execute the plan, he'd scrap it for one that was simpler, or one that was perhaps more dangerous to the whole, but that would ensure he'd get every man home. Likewise, "above all [his soldiers] trusted Ender to prepare them for anything and everything that might happen."

Bad leaders in *Ender's Game* and throughout history are consistently threatened by other people's competence. They luck into victory. They intimidate rather than motivate. Ender, on the other hand, seeks out intelligent subordinates and is confident enough not to have to be the best or smartest. He knows his abilities and the strengths and weaknesses of his team and seeks victory over adulation. In this sense, Ender is like one of the best bosses I ever had. This colonel knew his strengths and weaknesses. He sought out and hired the best officers to work for him instead of being threatened by them. He once told me that in every leadership position he's been in, he tried to hire people who were smarter than he was, and in every case it made his organization stand out from the rest.

It is a quirky truth that the leader who realizes that he is not the smartest and who seeks out the smartest to fill his ranks is in the end far wiser than the smart leader who can't stomach the thought of rising stars outshining him. During practice sessions, Ender often observes other commanders using "the hook" to move at will, but only during regularly scheduled practices. By using the hook, commanders ensure superiority of movement over their army members. This recognition gives Ender insight into the other commanders' rationale for only practicing on schedule: they need to be able to do something the other students can't do in order to maintain control.

Finally, and perhaps most significantly, Ender is humble. No matter how great his victory, no matter how thoroughly he vanquishes his opponents, he never gloats. He also never feels sorry for himself. Even when he stands up to Colonel Graff, it's not because he feels sorry for himself. He stands up to Graff to complain about injustice. When he is told plainly and directly that there is no justice in a survival fight, he accepts this as the truth and simply moves on to the next task. He learns quickly that the game is always on. Even before he discovers that the game is actually real combat, he knows that his fight against his own leadership is a continual game. That realization helps Ender accept that what he thought was a game was real war. The struggle against his commanders at Battle School is a game hidden within a broader game.

And so it is in America's military today. Let's consider the following passage:

They were career military, all of them. Proven officers with real ability. But in the military you don't
get trusted positions just because of your ability.
You also have to attract the notice of superior officers. You have to be liked. You have to fit in with
the system. You have to look like what the officers
above you think you should look like. You have to
think in ways that they are comfortable with.

The result was that you ended up with a command structure that was top-heavy with guys who
looked good in uniform and talked right and did
well enough not to embarrass themselves, while the
really good ones quietly did all the serious work
and bailed out their superiors and got blamed for
the errors they had advised against until they eventually got out.

That was the military.

These teachers were all the kind of people who
thrived in that environment. And they were select-
ing their favorite students based on precisely that
same screwed-up sense of priorities.

Over the last ten to fifteen years, passages like this
one have filled the pages of journals and magazines about
America's military. From the slowly building revolt at Fort
Leavenworth against Army leadership, best espoused by
then-Lieutenant Colonel Paul Yingling's "A Failure of Gen-
eralship," to articles on developing strategists and anti-
intellectualism in the armed forces, this passage is spot on.
Yet it was not written about America's military but about
Ender's own leadership, in *Ender's Shadow*.

Once officers understand this truth, then they have the responsibility to do something about it. A Pentagon leader recently directed one of his key colonels to figure out how to fundamentally change the culture of his service. But doing so would require an insurgency, a true fight against the service's own leadership for control over the service's direction. It is the same fight that Ender had to fight. Again, not some literary device, but a real insurgency.

And how is that fight turning out? We don't know yet, but it is not looking good. The members of any club determine its future membership. That means that to be promoted to general officer rank and have any meaningful impact on a population broader than a local unit, an officer must be selected by the generals above him for promotion. And human nature dictates that they select someone who is like them, someone who did the same things on the ladder of promotion. To select anyone else, anyone not like them, can only be seen as a self-repudiation, and that can never be allowed.

One officer recently selected for promotion to colonel told a retiring general that the service was in a mess and asked how it got that way. The general told him frankly that his own generation did not seize the opportunity given them to create change when the previous generation handed over the reins. The colonel asked what would happen next, and the general said that this new generation can and ought to effect a change, but in all likelihood they would take the more certain and easier road of doing nothing.

Ender sees this at the Battle School and afterwards. He recognizes the fundamental nature of humanity and knows that for every good intention, there is an evil one countering it. He does the best he can given what he has. He doesn't dwell on good or bad, right or wrong, when his life and humanity are on the line. Yet he knows that the betterment and survival of humanity is ultimately the greatest good and he goes about securing that the best way he can. His lessons ought to be taught and learned by not only science fiction readers but by the military as a whole and society in general.

Tom Ruby is a strategist, mentor, international speaker, and author. A retired Air Force colonel, he served in fighter wings, wrote Air Force doctrine, was the Associate Dean at the Air Command and Staff College, served twice on the Air Staff in the Pentagon, and deployed to combat assignments in the Middle East three times. He has spoken on leadership, critical thinking, and operational planning in England, France, Germany, and Poland as well as around the US.

Q. Knowing that Mazer Rackham stopped the second formic invasion by, basically, luck, why would IF want him to teach the more genius Ender?

A. Mazer Rackham did not rely on luck. He did not randomly fire a missile and happen to hit the right ship. He knew it was the right ship before he fired it.

He knew it was the right ship because he had the grand strategic vision to allow him to understand how the enemy was viewing her own forces and then discover the vantage point from which the enemy was seeing it all.

That ability to understand the enemy's mind is absolutely vital to successful command in war. Insane as he was, as long as Hitler understood his enemies and adapted his behavior accordingly, he was astonishingly successful against them; only when he did not comprehend them, as with the English and the Russian people, did he begin his march toward failure. Alexander, Caesar, Napoleon, and the other great warriors usually (though not always) shared this ability to accurately put themselves inside the enemy's mind, not consistently, but often enough to prevail.

This was why Mazer Rackham and no one else—was fit to be Ender's teacher in the end. Graff could teach him how to create and use his own forces, which is how Ender ended up with his superb jeesh, but only Mazer Rackham could teach him (or at least not interfere with his innate ability) to empathize with the opponent and thereby find a path to victory.

—OSC

Q. Why did the IF choose the same asteroid for IF Command that the formics chose for their base?

A. It was sheer practicality. The IF needed to be away from Earth in order to lure enemy attackers away from the home planet, to allow clarity of observation and communication without interference from an atmosphere, and to allow much coming-and-going of vehicles without the huge expense of overcoming planetary gravity. The formics had already turned Eros into an airtight, fully equipped installation; all the IF had to do was remodel a little, and then install their equipment. The formics had saved the IF years of work and billions of dollars. To the victor go the spoils.

—OSC

ENDER WIGGIN, USMC

JOHN F. SCHMITT

I knew Ender Wiggin very well. We were infantry captains together back in the day, stationed at the Marine Corps Warfighting Center during the Quantico Renaissance of the late 1980s and early 1990s. Of course, that's not true, the Quantico part anyway, although it might just as well have been.

I did know Ender Wiggin very well though. I have proof.

—

In the late 1980s and early 1990s, under the leadership of a visionary new Commandant, the US Marine Corps reinvented itself, adopting a radical new operational doctrine called Maneuver Warfare and implementing a bold and wide-ranging set of institutional changes to ensure it could execute that doctrine in war. Maneuver Warfare is based on tempo, surprise, boldness, trust relationships, ruthlessly attacking enemy vulnerabilities, and low-level commanders acting on their own initiative based on limited guidance from their seniors. (Dragon Army, anyone?) Given that a key tenet of Maneuver Warfare is leaders at all echelons exercising initiative on their own authority, developing those leaders became critically important. That period of change has sometimes been called the Maneuver Warfare Revolution, and because most of it revolved around Quantico, Virginia, it also has come to be known as the Quantico Renaissance. It was a heady time to be at Quantico, filled with intellectual energy and a compelling sense of purpose. I was there, a firebrand young captain who by good fortune had the opportunity to play a key role in those events.

Ender's Game also played no small role in helping to produce the changes that occurred, while reflecting perfectly the *zeitgeist* of the Marine Corps at that time. Let me assert this: *Ender's Game*, that brash little first novel about children by an author with no military experience, is an important work of military thought with much to offer the serious military professional. It is militarily significant because of what it has to say about three related subjects. First and foremost, *Ender's Game* is a book about the development of skilled military leaders, a topic critical to the successful implementation of Maneuver Warfare, as I said. It has insightful things to say about how to develop those leaders and the kinds of traits desirable in tacticians and strategists. Second, it is a thoughtful treatise on the nature of leadership, providing numerous examples both good and bad. Third, it offers the most compelling and accessible illustration of the theory and practice of Maneuver Warfare that exists—though, for reasons that will become clear, it pains me to say so.

Any Marine officer today would instantly recognize Ender Wiggin as a fellow Marine, a product of the Marine Corps training and education system (almost certainly an honor graduate) that grew out of the Quantico Renaissance. Any Marine would appreciate his leadership style and would intuitively recognize his tactics. Simply said, Ender Wiggin was a master practitioner of Maneuver Warfare. For myself, I felt like he was a brother in arms.

———

I received my commission as an officer of Marines, a brand-new second lieutenant, in 1981. I joined the service in the middle of an intense institutional debate, mostly played out on the pages of the *Marine Corps Gazette*, our professional journal, over how the post-Vietnam Marine Corps would approach the business of war. The Marine Corps had split into two opposing camps: the Maneuverists (who would eventually prove successful) and the Attritionists. The Maneuverists argued that the Attritionists favored mindlessly wearing the enemy down through firepower—the Vietnam "body count" mentality reborn. The Attritionists argued that the Maneuverists wanted to confuse the enemy to death, without actually fighting him.

After attending The Basic School and the Infantry Officers Course, I arrived at Camp Lejeune, North Carolina, in 1982 as a rifle platoon commander. Maj. Gen. Alfred M. Gray had just taken command of Second Marine Division there. Gray was a colorful, tobacco-chewing, gruff-talking, unconventional former enlisted Marine. He was also the leader of the Maneuver Warfare movement, which in the eyes of many made him a threat to the institution. Gray immediately pronounced Maneuver Warfare the official doctrine of Second Marine Division. I became an instant true believer, not only because Maneuver Warfare, with its emphasis on initiative at the lower echelons, was empowering to junior officers but also because everything I had read about the chaotic, uncertain, fluid, and temporal nature of war argued that Maneuver Warfare was the best approach.

I progressed from second lieutenant to captain in Second Marine Division. After about four years, I was assigned in 1986 to the Marine Corps Doctrine Center in Quantico, a sleepy little command that, to my eyes, at least was better than recruiting duty. I was the only captain in a building filled with unpromotable majors, lieutenant colonels, and colonels on their sunset tours. The debate over Maneuver Warfare was still raging, and I thought of myself as a Maneuver Warfare insurgent—I consciously did—within the belly of the beast, doing everything within my very limited power to reform the Marine Corps from the inside.

Then everything changed: in 1987, Al Gray—the outsider, the iconoclast, the threat to the institution— somehow got himself selected as the next Commandant of the Marine Corps. He immediately announced that Maneuver Warfare was the official doctrine of the Marine Corps and everybody had better get on board. Suddenly, everyone was a Maneuverist, and had been all along. Gray decided that he wanted a new manual to lay out his Maneuver Warfare philosophy. From my position of obscurity well down in the pecking order, I watched with amusement as colonels lined up around the block for a chance to audition for that gig.

For reasons I still don't understand—given that he didn't know my name—Gray picked me. I was going to work closely with the Commandant to capture his thoughts. Only it didn't happen that way. I never got any actual guidance. I met with Gray only twice, and each time he refused to talk about the book. Instead, he told sea stories. If I asked him a direct question, he'd tell me another sea story. He worked in parables. "Let me tell you a story about little Al Gray…," he'd growl. It was later that I realized he was actually practicing Maneuver Warfare; he was explaining his intent through those stories, but he was leaving it up to me —and *expecting* me—to figure out how to accomplish the mission. He was using what we called *trust tactics*, much as Ender did with Bean and other trusted subordinates.

The product was *Warfighting*, published in 1989. It described in seventy-seven pages the Marine Corps' view of the nature and challenges of war and how to win it. It was more a philosophy book than a typical military manual. *Warfighting* synthesized the works of Sun Tzu, Clausewitz, and John Boyd. Sun Tzu, the ancient Chinese general, wrote *The Art of War* around 450 BC. Clausewitz, the Prussian high priest of military theory, wrote *On War* after the Napoleonic Wars. Those works remain the two most important works of military theory in history. John Boyd, who died in 1997, was the most important American military theorist of the twentieth century.

Warfighting was well received. (It made my career and got me promoted to major two years ahead of schedule.)

In his foreword to the 1991 edition of *Ender's Game*, Orson Scott Card graciously called it "the most brilliant and concise book of military strategy ever written by an American." It became a centerpiece of instruction in all Marine Corps schools. It was translated into numerous foreign languages, including Chinese, which I always found ironic, given that so much of it was inspired by Sun Tzu. It was taught in foreign military academies. It has been published commercially several times, including as a leadership guide for business managers. (Because there had never been any public interest before in Marine Corps doctrinal publications, the Marine Corps did not bother to copyright it, so it was in the public domain.) You can buy it on Amazon. (I don't get a cent.)

The similarities between *Warfighting* and *Ender's Game* are manifold and uncanny: tempo, surprise, formlessness, ruthlessly attacking the enemy's critical vulnerabilities, exploiting fleeting opportunities, trust and implicit understanding between senior and subordinates, acceptance of risk, decisiveness, boldness, seizing the initiative, decentralization of authority, understanding the enemy and learning from him, knowing and inspiring your people—they are all there in spades.

Warfighting became probably the most lasting symbol of the Maneuver Warfare Revolution. The revised version (which I wrote in 1997) remains Marine Corps doctrine today. Looking back, I still feel pretty good about that book. I think it is a solid and readable description of Maneuver Warfare. In fact, I think there is only one book that captures Maneuver Warfare better: *Ender's Game*.

—

It was none other than John Boyd who turned me on to *Ender's Game*. A man of brilliant and hyper-disciplined intellect, Boyd was the intellectual powerhouse behind the military reform movement, and his theory provided the conceptual foundation for Maneuver Warfare. Boyd was a frequent lecturer in Quantico in those days. Although he had been an Air Force officer, the Air Force never really got him, and it was in the Marine Corps that his ideas really took hold. (Boyd's personal papers now reside in the archives at the Alfred M. Gray Research Center in Quantico.) Boyd's ideas came from everywhere—from history, literature, mathematics, classical and postmodern philosophy, sports, business management, economics, thermodynamics, quantum physics, and information theory—and, importantly for our purposes, science fiction.

So when John Boyd told me to read *Ender's Game*, though I did not think much of space opera as a rule, I dutifully went out and bought a copy. (So did a lot of other Marine officers: the book was a cult classic in the Marine Corps long before it reached the universal popularity it enjoys today.) I can't say I began to read it with super-high expectations, however. Needless to say, that changed pretty quickly.

This was 1989, shortly after I had written *Warfighting*. As soon as I started reading *Ender's Game*, I realized it was brilliant—and absolutely relevant to what was happening in the Marine Corps at that time. I felt an instant connection, like Orson Scott Card had taken the ideas of *Warfighting* and converted them into a novel. About that time, Brig. Gen. P.K. Van Riper, one of Gray's leading revolutionaries, was transforming the Marine Corps University (MCU) from a collection of staff training schools teaching planning procedures to a genuine university developing thinking leaders. One of the first steps was to offer a series of evening courses to anybody stationed at Quantico. I decided to teach "Introduction to Maneuver Warfare" or Maneuver Warfare 101. I targeted junior officers and enlisted Marines. I ran the course as a seminar, based on a lot of practical decision exercises rather than a lot of reading. I assigned only three books: *Warfighting* (of course), Sun Tzu's *The Art of War*, and *Ender's Game*.

I also decided, as soon as I had read *Ender's Game*, that I needed to bring Orson Scott Card to Quantico. The question was how to find him. Remember, this was in the days before people searches on the internet. I guess I could have written to his publisher, but I didn't have that kind of patience. That was okay, though, because I knew where he lived. Recall that when Ender graduated from the Battle School after defeating Griffin and Tiger armies without a fight, they sent him to Greensboro, North Carolina, for rest and relaxation with his sister, Valentine. On page 133 of my copy, I have written "Greensboro!!!" in the margin. I looked up the area code, called directory assistance, asked for Orson Scott Card's number, and, before I knew it, was being connected.

I hadn't figured out what I was going to say when he answered. I stammered out an introduction and launched into some spiel about the military virtues of *Ender's Game*. Capt. John Kuntz, a colleague, walked in. I put my hand over the mouthpiece and said: "I can't believe I'm talking to Orson

Scott Card about *Ender's Game.*" Unbeknownst to me, Scott was on the other end telling his wife, Kristine: "I can't believe I'm talking to a Marine captain about *Ender's Game.*"

It turned out Scott was teaching a writing workshop in the DC area soon and was able to extend his trip to drive down to Quantico for a day. The Marine Corps does pomp and ceremony like nobody's business. We gave Scott quite the reception. First stop was a meet-and-greet with the faculty of the Command and Staff College, the senior school of the Marine Corps University—Gen. Van Riper and about fifteen to twenty lieutenant colonels and colonels, each with his own copy of the book to be signed. Imagine a bunch of tough-as-nails Marine officers gushing over a science fiction writer. We immediately launched into a discussion of the book, which I don't think Scott was expecting. *Speaker for the Dead* had come out in paperback by that time, and a lot of the faculty had read that too, so we jumped into a discussion of it as well.

We made the rounds of the other schools—the Amphibious Warfare School (AWS, for captains), The Basic School (TBS, for all lieutenants, where they learned how to be Marine officers before moving on to their specialty schools), and the Staff NCO Academy (for senior enlisted Marines). Each place we visited, it was the same: the Rock Star Treatment.

The highlight of the visit was the seminar with my Introduction to Maneuver Warfare class that evening. The group was twice its normal size, as a lot of other faculty, including Gen. Van Riper again, sat in for an extremely animated discussion on Ender Wiggin as a military leader and tactician. We attacked that book like … well, like a platoon of Marines assaulting a hill. We took no prisoners. It was Scott's first exposure to US Marines, and I don't think he was quite prepared for what he got. He put up a good fight, but in the end, as I recall, he was just overrun.

—

One of the fundamentally important ideas in *Ender's Game* is the notion of games as an instrument for training military commanders. The soldiers in *Ender's Game* are children, and children naturally play games, so this might seem like a trivial insight. But I think it is actually a profound thought. Play can be serious business, as *Ender's Game* captures very well. This idea is also part of the Maneuver Warfare philosophy.

The most important training tenet of Maneuver Warfare is that exercises (our name for war games) should be free-play—that is, neither side is constrained in what they can do—just as the war games at the Battle School were. This replicates the fundamental nature of war as a clash between two hostile and *independent* forces unconstrained by any rules. As Mazer Rackham tells Ender the first time they meet: "And the only rules of the game are what you can do to him and what you can stop him from doing to you." You would think this would be obvious, but it was not how the Marine Corps approached training Before Gray. Typically, a training exercise involved an exercise force, which was the unit being trained, and an OPFOR, which was there to serve as training aids for the exercise force. The OPFOR was always outnumbered. It was not allowed to do anything unpredictable but instead was expected to fall back— fall back and eventually die in place. In other words, the OP-FOR was expected to cooperate in its own defeat, which meant that the exercise force did not need to think about tactics but could just focus on getting its own procedures right. This led to an inward focus, which was the opposite of Maneuver Warfare's outward focus on the enemy.

The other games connection between *Ender's Game* and Maneuver Warfare is what the Marine Corps came to call Tactical Decision Games (TDGs for short, because everything in the military can be reduced to a three-letter abbreviation, including "three letter abbreviation" or TLA). TDGs are concise (less than five hundred words), deceptively simple scenarios that build up to a tactical dilemma requiring an immediate command decision. They start with the words "You are the commander of…" to drive home the point that you and nobody else is responsible. (Moral, as well as physical, courage is a critical attribute of command.) TDGs include a simple map showing the terrain and where your forces are. You are given a mission. You are given some information about the enemy situation but never as much as you think you need. Then, usually, something unexpected happens, rendering your orders obsolete, so you have to come up with a new plan on the spot. A good TDG has built-in time pressure, usually severe—for example, if you do not act within two minutes, an approaching enemy patrol will spot your whole formation and you will lose the element of surprise. If a TDG is designed well, your instinctive reaction is a sinking feeling in the pit of your stomach and the thought: "What the heck do I do now?"

Your solution has to take the form of the actual orders you would issue to your units, plus a sketch of your plan. In other words, there's no academic discussion about this or that course of action; you have to take responsibility and act. The important thing is not the actual tactics you use, although some are better than others. The goal is to improve tactical decision-making, so the important thing is *why* you did what you did. TDGs are best done in a small-group setting, led by an experienced tactician, where you can discuss these things and benefit from other people's decisions. We also developed "double-blind" TDGs, a more interactive, turn-based version in which two teams each solve the same tactical problem from opposing sides, with a controller moving between the two teams presenting each team with a new problem based on the other team's last decision. We have since developed interactive, online versions.

But back then we were still figuring out the basic uses and mechanisms of TDGs. Here, my own professional journey intersects the narrative. Before being assigned to Quantico, I had had the good fortune to command two different infantry companies in Second Marine Division. I was still a junior captain when I wrote *Warfighting*, and I fully expected to get another company when I returned to the operating forces. I thought of myself as a company commander, as a tactician. As I was writing *Warfighting*, I remember thinking: "With everything I'm learning, I'm going to be one hotshot company commander when I get back to the Fleet." Only it didn't work out that way. Don't get me wrong; writing *Warfighting* was an unbelievable education. But I realized pretty quickly that none of it was making me a better company commander. The deeper I dug into the theory, the more abstract it got and the further away I got from actual application. From a very personal point of view, I needed something to make Maneuver Warfare more concrete. My circle of insurgents at MCU was dealing with a similar dilemma: how to make Maneuver Warfare theory more accessible to most Marines. We just hadn't broken the code yet.

There was another group of Maneuver Insurgents that used to meet in the evenings at the Marine Barracks in Washington, DC, and I sometimes made the drive up from Quantico. One night, Bill Lind, one of the leading civilians in the broader military reform movement on Capitol Hill, invited Brig. Gen. Hasso von Uslar, the military attaché from the West German Embassy, as a guest speaker. At one point during the evening, we were debating some tactical issue (I don't recall what it was anymore). As a way to ground the discussion, von Uslar pulled out a map, indicated a couple of positions, and said: "How would you do it on this piece of terrain?" It was a revelation to me. It had instantly turned the abstract discussion concrete. It was a proto-TDG at best, still with the format and mechanics to be worked out, but I realized immediately we had found what we were looking for. I drove home that evening and worked into the night to draft what became the first TDG, "Enemy Over the Bridge." It is reproduced in the adjacent sidebar.

My cabal of insurgents back at MCU debated what to call this new invention. Normally, in the military such training activities are called "exercises." There are field exercises (FEXes), map exercises (MAPEXes), and command post exercises (CPXes). But we decided we wanted a different vibe.

We wanted to market these things as fun, so Marines would be encouraged to do them, to *play* them. So we very deliberately decided on Tactical Decision *Games*. (We all had read *Ender's Game* by that time; I don't recall that the book, and its title, actually entered into the discussion, but I have no doubt it influenced us subconsciously at least).

We formed The TDG Group at MCU. With Gen. Van Riper's permission, we quit work early every Friday afternoon and met in the conference room to play TDGs for a couple hours. Sometimes he joined us. Everybody was invited. We got mostly officers, but some enlisted Marines and even some civilians showed up. Each week, two or three people were responsible for bringing new TDGs for the group to play and leading the discussion on their own scenarios. We experimented with different formats for presenting a scenario and different techniques for leading the discussion. Then we started exporting TDGs to the various schools, teaching the instructors how to author them and lead the discussions. The Basic School took the desks out of one of their large classrooms and replaced them with sand tables so brand-new lieutenants could do TDGs on three-dimensional terrain. I made TDGs the centerpiece of my Maneuver Warfare 101 course.

I submitted "Enemy Over the Bridge" to the *Marine Corps Gazette*, not sure what the editors would make of an article that wasn't really an article. They published it in the April 1990 issue and solicited solutions from the readers. We got more than a hundred submissions. One was sketched on a C-Ration carton, as it might expediently have been done in the field. TDGs had struck a nerve. They became a regular feature in the *Gazette*, with a new game published each month and selected solutions published two months later. The *Gazette's* editor-in-chief, Col. John Greenwood, became a regular member of The TDG Group. To this day, TDGs remain an integral part of Marine Corps culture and one of the most indelible reminders of the Maneuver Warfare Revolution.

—

Reading also was a critical part of the Maneuver Warfare Revolution. All Marines now were expected to read regularly as part of their professional development. One of my final duties before being transferred from Quantico in the summer of 1990 was to help put together the Commandant's Reading List, which assigned titles by rank and category (strategy, tactics, logistics, leadership, etc.). I edited what became known as the *Book on Books*, a catalog of all the titles, with a synopsis of each. One of my first acts was to make sure *Ender's Game* got on the list. This is the entry I wrote for the first *Book on Books*:

> **Card, Orson Scott.** *Ender's Game* (New York, NY: St. Martin's Press)
>
> **Cpl/Sgt; Tactics**
>
> This is the story of the development of a military genius in the guise of clever, brash, exhilarating, and extremely enjoyable science fiction. Even if you do not like science fiction, you will love this book—and you will learn a lot in the process. Alien "buggers" have already unsuccessfully attacked the earth

and are coming back for another try. Outnumbered and ill-equipped, the earth leaders know the only hope of survival rests in finding a military genius who can outfight the buggers. They choose young Ender Wiggin, and his intense training comes in the form of space-age war games. Ender thinks he is but one student among many, but the administrators of the battle school have a particular curriculum in mind for the young soldier, who will be put to the severest test. The tactics Ender develops in his training are based on fluidity, adaptability, tempo, deception, ambiguity, and a keen appreciation for the enemy. If this sounds remarkably similar to maneuver warfare, it is.

I like to think I was personally responsible for the sale of thousands of copies of *Ender's Game*. It is hard to find a Marine of my generation who is not intimately familiar with the book, and to this day, if you were to describe someone as "an Ender," you would be hard-pressed to find a Marine who did not know exactly what you mean. The term has found its way into the professional jargon.

The Marine Corps University has produced no less than three discussion guides for leaders to use while discussing *Ender's Game* in a group setting as part of a professional military education program in their units. Two are available online at:

- http://www.mcu.usmc.mil/lejeune_leadership/ LLI%20Documnets/Enders%20Game%201.pdf
- http://www.mcu.usmc.mil/lejeune_leadership/ LLI%20Documnets/Enders%20Game%202.pdf

I quote from the third of these to provide an idea of the professional topics that Marines explore through *Ender's Game*:

> *Leadership*: How many different kinds of leaders can you find in the book? What advantages and disadvantages do they have? What is it about the most effective leaders in the story that seems to set them above the rest of the pack? Does this reflect your experience? How do we define leadership and evaluate some of the leaders in the book such as Colonel Graff, Mazer Rackham, Bonzo Madrid, Rose the Nose, Petra, Bean, Peter, and Valentine?
>
> *Training and team-building*: What is different about how Battle School does training and education than what we see in the military? Why is this? What features of military training and education should be in Battle School? What features in Battle School should be in the military? How is conflict between leaders and followers, between leaders, and between followers handled? What seems to be the glue that holds cohesive teams together and makes them effective inside and outside the Battle Room? What tears teams apart?
>
> *Maneuver Warfare/Tactics*: What is it about Ender's method that contributes to his tactical success in and outside of the Battle Room? Why do other armies and leaders fail when he succeeds? Card has much to say about the role of "extra practice," trust between leaders and team members, innovation, and non-formulaic approaches/unpredictability.

As that discussion guide notes, *"Ender's Game* is about more than the difficulty and excitement that competition provides in preparing for combat. There are lessons in training methodology, leadership, and ethics as well. Such richness in range and treatment has made Card's book an oft-read and re-read title for many years; *Ender's Game* has been a stalwart item on the Marine Corps Reading List since its inception."

—

That evening in Quantico in early 1990, when Scott Card visited, my Maneuver Warfare 101 class broke Ender Wiggin down as a commander, analyzed the heck out of him. I argued that the essence of what made him a great commander was that Ender, a "Third," combined the dominant traits of his two older siblings. Obviously, all three Wiggin children were extremely intelligent, which always helps. But what was critical was that Ender merged Peter's ruthless cruelty with Valentine's extreme empathy. Alone, each trait was disqualifying, and so Peter and Valentine both eventually were deemed unsuitable as potential commanders. But the merging of those traits in Ender was the critical element for potential greatness.

Always very self-aware (another valuable trait in a commander), Ender comes to recognize that trait in himself. Granted leave back in Greensboro after graduating from the Battle School, he has an exchange with Valentine. He says:

> "In the moment when I truly understand my enemy, understand him well enough to defeat him, then in that very moment I also love him. I think

it's impossible to really understand somebody, what they want, what they believe, and not love them the way they love themselves. And then, in that very moment when I *love* them—"

"You beat them." For a moment she was not afraid of his understanding.

"No, you don't understand. I *destroy* them. I make it impossible for them to ever hurt me again. I grind them and grind them until they don't *exist*."

(In perhaps the most famous line from *The Art of War*, Sun Tzu says: "Know the enemy and know yourself; in a hundred battles you will never be in peril.")

That short exchange between Ender and Valentine, I argued, was the central revelation and the most important passage of the entire book, in which you get the essence of what makes Ender Wiggin a brilliant commander. (You also, of course, get the starting point for *Speaker*.)

Even Ender's name is revealing of this character trait. We are told that Andrew Wiggin is called "Ender" from a very young age because Valentine mispronounces "Andrew." That is a nice literary device, but I always felt it was more than a little transparent. "Ender" is not merely a name; it is a fundamental description of Wiggin as a tactician. He is very much an ender: exploiting that gift for utterly ruthless empathy, he goes decisively for the heart of each situation to finish it quickly. "Ender" is fundamentally both who and what he is.

After Ender has defeated the formics in the climactic battle, Mazer Rackham says: "You made the hard choice, boy. All or nothing. *End them or end us*." [Emphasis mine.]

As Sun Tzu said: "Hence what is essential in war is victory, not prolonged operations."

This idea of *ending*, which Card captures so compellingly as a character trait, continuously occupies every military commander and theorist as a matter of military theory, namely: how best to take apart an enemy? Sun Tzu said: "Should one ask: 'How do I cope with a well-ordered enemy host about to attack me?' I reply: 'Seize something he cherishes and he will conform to your desires.'" Clausewitz called it the *center of gravity*:

> [O]ne must keep the dominant characteristics of both belligerents [i.e., the two opposing sides] in mind. Out of those characteristics, a certain center of gravity develops, the hub of all power and movement, on which everything depends. That is the point against which all our energies should be directed.

While Clausewitz explores the source of a combatant's strength, *Warfighting* chooses to approach from the direction of a combatant's weakness, using the term *critical vulnerability*:

> So we seek to strike the enemy where, when, and how he is most vulnerable…Of all the vulnerabilities we might choose to exploit, some are more critical to the enemy than others. It follows that the most effective way to defeat our enemy is to destroy that which is most critical to him. We should focus our efforts on the one thing which, if eliminated, will do the most decisive damage to his ability to resist us.

I think this formulation is the one closest to Ender's own thinking. This thought always seems to be foremost in his mind whenever he is in a fight. Granted, he offers a rational explanation for acting this way in each case, whether through his inner thoughts or later explanation, but I believe that is mere rationalization. I think ruthlessly exploiting the critical vulnerability is an intrinsic part of his character. He does it time and again. It is, literally, who he is.

Scott insisted he had none of these ideas in mind when he wrote *Ender's Game*. Right.

—

Anyway, I began by saying that I knew Ender Wiggin very well.

After that long day at Quantico, when the faculty at the Marine Corps University treated Scott Card like a rock star and my Maneuver Warfare 101 class had the privilege of dissecting *Ender's Game* with the author, Scott signed my marked-up, dog-eared paperback copy. He wrote: "To John Schmitt—A man who understood Ender better than I did—Scott."

Nice of him to say, although manifestly not true, of course. Still, I consider it one of the finest compliments of my professional career.

John F. Schmitt was commissioned a second lieutenant in the US Marines after graduating from Northwestern University in June 1981. He spent four years as an infantry commander in the Second Marine Division in Camp Lejeune, North Carolina. In 1986, he was assigned to the Doctrine Center in Quantico, Virginia, where he wrote the keystone Marine Corps doctrinal manuals Ground Combat Operations, Warfighting, *and* Campaigning. *He left active duty in 1993 and is self-employed as a military consultant and writer. He resides in Champaign, Illinois, with his wife and three children.*

TDG 90-1

"ENEMY OVER THE BRIDGE"

The following is an example of a tactical deci-
sion game like those in use at the Marine Corps
University as a tool for developing military judg-
ment and decision-making ability. The basic
idea behind these deceptively simple games is to
create a hypothetical battlefield dilemma of some
sort and require the players to develop a solution
under pressure of a time limit. The games work
best in groups of up to about a dozen, where
Marines can argue the merits of various plans.
The games are designed to teach students how
to think rather than what to think, the rationale
being that because each situation is unique, it
is futile to try to provide the right answer in ad-
vance for every conceivable situation. There are
no absolute right or wrong answers. As long as a
solution reflects the tenets of Maneuver Warfare,
it is the "right" answer.

THE SITUATION

You are the commanding officer, Third Battalion, Sixth Marines. Your battalion consists of a
scout platoon, two tank companies (A and C),

and two mechanized infantry companies (B and D). Friendly forces hold the bridge and the riverline to the west. (Intelligence reports the river is unfordable.) Friendly reconnaissance elements are operating west of the river. Tomorrow morning the division begins a major offensive west across the river, with the division's main effort in Sixth Marines' zone. Your battalion will spearhead the regiment's attack.

You are to occupy the assembly area south of Hamlet in preparation for the morning attack across the river commencing at 0400. You

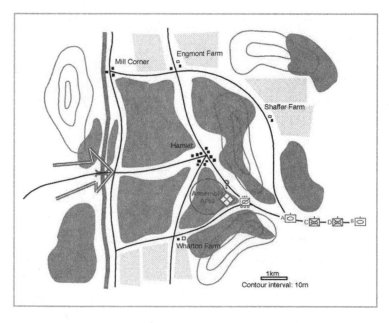

Originally published in Marine Corps Gazette, *April 1990. The scenario has been simplified slightly from the original.*

are moving northwest toward the assembly area as shown. At 2000, your scout platoon, which is forward reconnoitering the route, reports enemy infantry occupying your assembly area in strength and continuing to reinforce. The size of the enemy force is unknown but estimated to be at least a company. Further, the scout platoon commander reports he has just met an allied reconnaissance team that was operating west of the river but has been forced east across the river under fire. The reconnaissance team leader reports there is no sign of friendly forces holding the riverline or the bridge and that enemy infantry with some light vehicles and tanks has been moving across the bridge for at least thirty minutes. This is all the information your scout commander can tell you.

As the battalion commander, what will you do?

REQUIREMENT

Within a five-minute time limit, give your solution in the form of the fragmentary order you will issue to your subordinates—to include the intent behind your plan—and support it with an overlay sketch.

ONE SOLUTION TO "ENEMY OVER THE BRIDGE"

This was my original solution to "Enemy Over the Bridge," published in the *Marine Corps Gazette*, with three other solutions, June 1990.

BATTALION COMMANDER'S ORDER

"The battalion attacks *immediately* to seize the bridge in order to cut off the flow of enemy forces east and to secure a bridgehead for the division's attack at 0400 tomorrow. Scout platoon: Move west toward Wharton Farm to clear the engagement area and determine enemy dispositions along that axis. Charlie will be attacking from your rear, so imperative you clear the vicinity of the assembly area. Alpha Company, with Delta in trace: Attack the bridge as rapidly as possible via Engmont Farm to sever the enemy movement east and secure the bridgehead. You are the main effort. Charlie: Probe west in order to determine size of enemy force and contain it in the assembly area. Develop the situation based on your estimate, but do not become decisively engaged. Most important, keep the enemy force fixed where it is. Bravo: You are reserve. Take up position near Engmont Farm, prepared to reinforce Alpha and Delta or attack south toward Hamlet to destroy the enemy."

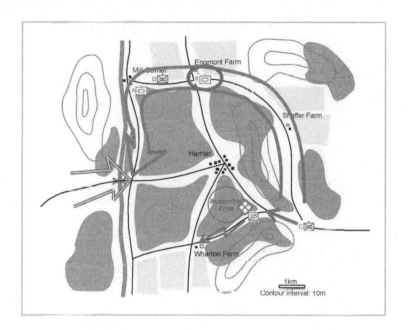

Contour interval: 10m

EXPLANATION

Occupying the assigned assembly area is no longer relevant since the situation has changed dramatically. Although the enemy in the assembly area may be the immediate problem, the more critical problem is the situation at the bridge. To keep a potentially bad situation from getting worse and to facilitate the division's offensive launching on time, I must secure the bridge. The situation in the assembly area is too obscure to commit to a decisive engagement—nor is it important at this stage to do that—although I do want to develop the situation there. My scout platoon is a problem: they are caught between the enemy and Charlie Company with a fight about to break out. I have to extract them without exposing them to Charlie's fire. By pushing them west, I get them out of the way and I use them for their primary mission of gaining information about the situation. I soon will have information about the situation on the northern flank from Alpha and Delta; I have no other means of getting information about the situation on the southern flank. The location of my reserve, Bravo Company, at Engmont Farm protects my route to the bridge and allows me both to reinforce quickly toward the bridge and to attack toward Hamlet, although I realize it is out of position if I need it in the south.

Q. There is another side to the story I've wanted to know. What is the story behind the pilots and officers of the invasion force in *Ender's Game*? As a reader, knowing Ender, Bean, Dink, Petra, and the others, it would be extremely interesting to see the battles from the invasion force's point of view. Was the faith of the other pilots shaken when Petra's group was temporarily paralyzed by her meltdown? What was going through the pilots' minds when face-to-face and hopelessly outnumbered in their last encounter? All of them more or less plummeted to the formic home world without regard for themselves.

A. Remember that the pilots in the final battle had information that the pilots who fought the early battles did not: They had seen Ender win battle after battle. By this point they had absolute faith in his ability.

At the same time, they also knew that the other pilots' victories in all the previous battles meant nothing if this last fleet was beaten at the formics' home world.

They could see how many formic ships there were; they could imagine a fleet like this surrounding Earth. Though everyone they knew back home was already old or dead, they still had loyalty to the world and the human race they had so recently left, and whose only protection they were.

There are many examples of courageous soldiers making assaults like this one, with little chance of individual survival, for the sake of carrying the overall battle. Countless examples of small groups fighting to the last man to buy time for a larger group to get away, regroup, or prepare to counterattack.

At the same time, we have plenty of examples of otherwise brave soldiers openly mutinying rather than obey orders that would lead to pointless slaughter. The 1917 mutiny in the French Army in World War I arose because the poilus were sick of being commanded to charge machine guns, using the same bankrupt tactics over and over to the same empty end.

Yet in thinking of that mutiny, it is good to remember that it took place in 1917—after nearly three years of the same pointless massacre with every assault against the German lines. The poilus did not mutiny until they had seen more than a million of their comrades die or get maimed or gassed in previous assaults. How many times did they obey those absurd, wicked, wasteful orders with great courage, before they finally said, *Enough—stop wasting our lives.*

So it was that combination—a knowledge that they were the last defense and hope of the human race, and a trust that if anyone could make their sacrifice amount to something, it was Ender Wiggin—that motivated them to "go over the top" in the face of overwhelming enemy fire.

They also knew what weapons they were carrying. They knew that if they got close enough to the massed fleet, the M.D. Device would create a destructive field that would feed on the mass of every ship it destroyed, and leap from ship to ship, perhaps all the way around the planet. They did not realize that Ender hoped to destroy the planet itself, and create a field that would wipe out everything, so there was no hope of the formics ever rising again from the cinders of this world. But they did understand that they had the capability of devastatingly effective attack. So they knew that Ender Wiggin was not throwing them against the enemy "machine guns" just to demonstrate courage or honor; this was no charge of the light brigade. They knew that if they got the M.D. Device into the midst of the enemy, victory might be achieved.

There was also no anonymity. No one could slip away unnoticed, even if inclined to do so. Therefore any lack of courage would also bring open shame in the eyes of friends who *were* obeying orders.

Under such circumstances, such men will and do sacrifice their lives, and have done so many times in the past. In this I know human nature well enough, and have enough history behind me, to feel absolute confidence that well-led soldiers will act as these soldiers acted, without a single man holding back or refusing to go.

—OSC

Q. Some would argue that *Ender's Game* encourages critical thinking within the military, others argue that it glorifies war. Response to both?

A. The former is absolutely true; the latter absurdly wrong.

Peacetime military organizations promote bureaucrats to high command. It usually takes failures and defeats to identify the deadwood and get rid of it. Think of Lincoln's search for a competent commander for the Army of the Potomac in the Civil War. Everyone thought he had that commander in McClellan, but in fact McClellan was the ultimate peacetime general: all training and maneuver, but unwilling to commit to battle. It took a long time to realize that McClellan was not a war commander and to replace him with someone who was.

Military organizations get themselves locked into mindsets that they cannot break free of. The "cult of the offensive" in World War I killed millions of soldiers by running them up against machine guns; not until Churchill's tanks, and the fresh American military, changed the equation did victory become possible, and even then, most generals on both sides had utterly failed to learn the obvious lessons being taught in blood and horror on the battlefield.

In *Ender's Game*, Graff and the others committed to Battle School understood that peacetime and doctrinaire commanders could not be weeded out in combat; they had to be weeded out in advance. This is part of what Mazer and Graff work out in the story "Mazer in Prison." Victory will not be possible if the commander is chosen according to the normal pattern; creative, risk-taking leadership must be in place from the start, because there will be no time, no slack, in which to discover the real commanders after a few failures. There can *be* no failures.

This is much of the reason why military readers respond well to *Ender's Game*. No one understands better than soldiers and officers how hard it is to get the right commander in the right place to achieve victory. Only a military that is able to self-criticize, learn from mistakes, and replace misplaced commanders has any chance of achieving its goals, especially when facing an opponent that *does* recognize errors, learn from them, and move incompetent leaders out of positions where lives and outcomes depend on their decisions.

As to "glorifying war," what is invariably meant by this is that I show excellent soldiers as good people worthy of respect. The kind of people who complain about "glorifying war" are almost always people who think they're "anti-war," when they're merely ignorant of history. When an aggressive enemy is determined to make war on you, then the only choices are to resist militarily or accept the aggressors as your overlords.

After the fall of France in World War II—a fall that was not necessary, had the French been competently led, for the Germans could have been defeated at several points after the breakthrough in the Ardennes—there were still many among the governing elite in Britain who, because of their hatred of war, were prepared to make peace with Hitler. It was only Churchill, who understood the indomitable will of the people, who kept Britain from surrender. *Any* other likely candidate for Prime Minister at that time would certainly have sued for peace.

What would have been the result? Quite possibly a Europe dominated even today by either Nazism or Stalinism, or their successors. *There are worse things*

than war. To recognize this is not "glorifying war"—it is recognizing that the best
way to avoid war is to appear irresistibly
strong and resolute to those who consider attacking you.

A resolute Britain, led in 1935 by the
"warmonger" Churchill or one of the few
who agreed with him, would certainly
have avoided World War II and brought
about the fall of Hitler at very little cost.
It was the people who hated war and refused to arm for it who allowed Hitler to
rise to domination of Western Europe.

It is tragic but true that war can never
be avoided by the unilateral decision not
to arm or fight. The only result of such a
decision is that the other side will win.

However, it is also true that there *is*
such a thing as glorifying war as witnessed in the attitude of many nations
prior to World War I. But in this case, they
were delusional about what war is: They
had in mind the quick German victory in
the Franco-Prussian War, or the tidy little
colonial wars Britain had a habit of winning at very little cost (though the Boer
War *should* have been a wakeup call, as it
was not tidy nor quick nor low-cost).

Even then, what was needed was not
an *anti-military* attitude, but a cold-blooded understanding of the brutal and terrible cost of war and a sharp eye toward
what the goals of war should be. The fact
is that not one of the nations that began

World War I had anything meaningful to gain by victory, and all of them had much to lose through defeat.

Ender's Game does not glorify war in the way that it was glorified in the imaginations of those who decided to move ahead toward war in 1914. On the contrary, if anything, *Ender's Game* shows with brutal clarity just what war costs those who fight it, so that even when war is necessary, only a fool goes into it joyfully.

Yet when war cannot be avoided, when the cost of not-fighting becomes too high to be borne, one hopes that the military has been treated with respect and given the resources and training that allow them to serve their purpose and go to war with a reasonable prospect of victory. That is *respecting and supporting the military*, not glorifying war. It is unfortunate that many short-sighted people confuse the two ideas.

—*OSC*

Q. Was there any particular reason you assigned Dragon Army the colors grey, orange, grey?

A. No.

—*OSC*

THE PRICE OF OUR INHERITANCE

NEAL SHUSTERMAN

was lucky enough to run into Orson Scott Card at a recent conference, and over lunch we discussed the nature of the essays coming in for the collection. He found it interesting, and often flattering that people felt compelled to reminisce about where and when they first read *Ender's Game*, as if it were the memorable shedding of their virginity. I, of course, won't go there. You'll never catch me talking about my first time.[1]

My curiosity was piqued by the conversation, though, because it pointed to the interesting fact that people *do*

---

[1] I was sitting on the floor in the hallway of a hotel while on vacation. I had to be out in the hallway because I didn't want to wake the baby or my wife, who had tired of hearing me flip pages of *Ender's Game* in bed.

remember details around their first reading of *Ender's Game*, in the same way people remember profound, life-changing events. For instance, so many of us remember exactly what we were doing the moment we heard about planes hitting the Twin Towers, or—for those of us who are parents— where we were the day we first learned we were going to be a father or mother. In time, our lives become slideshows of events that have left an indelible imprint on us. They be- come larger than life in our memories—and reading *Ender's Game* is quite often a larger-than-life event.

I've read many memorable books, but few of them have such gravity that the memory sucks in other events around it like a black hole. I asked a number of friends, and dis- covered that each of them had also experienced "The Full Ender." They proceeded to give me amazingly specific de- tails about the first time their minds were subverted into thinking about formics, Battle School, and all that went with them.[2]

A common thread was that everyone—*everyone*— claimed they had been kept up until four o'clock in the morning reading. I have determined that 4:00 AM is the golden hour of great literature, because, let's face it, any- one can stay up until three o'clock reading—and a book that keeps you up until 5:00 AM? Well, that's just annoying. But reading until the fourth hour—that is the sign of truly great literature. So, regardless of the facts, if your *memory*

---

[2] It was more of a bed and breakfast than a hotel. The hallway in which I was reading had green carpet and yellow walls, and it smelled of dusty potpourri that infused the pages of the book.

tells you that you were up until four o'clock in the morning reading, then it must have been a life-altering book.

The question is: What makes *Ender's Game* a fourth-hour book? What is it that we find so compelling? Certainly it's the strength of character and story, but I think it goes beyond that to a deeper, more primal place. In Ender's journey, Orson Scott Card has tapped into a visceral human conundrum: the ambivalence of survival.

—

"If you can't beat them then they deserve to win, because they're stronger and better than us."
—Valentine Wiggin

—

Evolution is cruel. Life is constantly in brutal conflict. Species evolve only through the untimely death of the weak and the unadaptable. *Homo sapiens*, however, as the apex species, has the luxury of compassion and empathy. We humans care deeply for the less fortunate. We are charitable souls, helping the needy and the infirmed. We seek cures for congenital diseases, refusing to allow nature the vicious victory of killing off a gene by slaying its sufferers. Instead, we find courage and meaning in their struggle far more than the struggle of the hunter over its prey. To modern man, survival doesn't mean eat or be eaten, kill or be killed; it means a regular paycheck, a retirement fund, and a mortgage that isn't upside down.

But what happens when it's more than our mortgage that's upside down? What do we become if survival truly becomes about survival once more? We would all like to think that we are enlightened beings and, as such, will always find the moral high road. Wisdom tells us the path is more important than the destination. However, when survival is truly at stake, suddenly the destination is everything, regardless of the path we take to get there.

—

> *"No, you don't understand. I destroy them. I make it impossible for them ever to hurt again. I grind them and grind them until they don't exist."*
>
> —ENDER WIGGIN

—

Tell me—would you ever kill your neighbor in cold blood? No, you say? Well, what if it was to save your life? Still no? Then what if it was to save the lives of your children?

A parent knows that that's not even the right question. The right question is, *How* many *people would you kill to protect the lives of your children?* And every parent also knows the answer:

As many as necessary.

So ... if the survival of your family, your race, your species depended entirely on the irrevocable destruction of another species, would you pull the trigger on Dr. Device?

The threat from the formics was spelled out clearly. They attacked twice. The first attack was an exploratory mission; the second attack was an attempt to colonize. On both occasions, it was clear that they meant to destroy humanity, and there was no reason to think that they would stop. So, how was humanity going to save its children? How many formics would we kill? As many as necessary. Even if it meant every last one of them.

—

"Killing's the first thing we learned. And it's a good thing we did, or we'd be dead, and tigers would own the earth."

—Valentine Wiggin

—

The real power of *Ender's Game* is that it's not just about Ender's mission—it's about each of us coming to terms with that basic kill-or-be-killed imperative that Valentine so plainly put forth. At its most primal level, *Ender's Game* is about the decisions we make as human beings when faced with dire circumstances, and why we make them. It also lays bare the ugly truth that species survival sometimes trumps compassion and empathy. Ender becomes for us the embodiment of this unthinkable question. *What if, for humanity to survive, we as a species must surrender the very things that make us human?*

However, to embody the question, he must also embody the answer—which he does by being more than just a victor, but the ultimate game-changer. When he couldn't win by following the rules, he found ways around the rules without actually breaking them. Part of what makes him so compelling is that he finds loopholes no one else is smart enough to find—and the greatest of these circumnavigations is that he performs the unthinkable act of xenocide without ever losing his humanity. Ender gives us a noble answer to the question: No, we do not have to surrender our humanity to survive. Ender keeps his humanity, so perhaps we can, too.

When I first read *Ender's Game* many years ago,[3] there was a single review quote from the back cover that stuck in my mind. It said, *Ender's Game* was "a scathing indictment of the military mind." It bothered me. I wasn't quite sure why at first. I wondered if that's what the author intended—because it felt "off." Incomplete. I ultimately came to realize that the book was ambivalent like Ender himself. *Ender's Game* is both an indictment *and* a vindication of militaristic thinking at the same time. It provides a quandary, not a position. *Ender's Game* does not give us a moral neatly wrapped with a bow—instead it opens the drawstring on a nasty bag of questions.

Take Graff, for instance. Is he a monster or a hero? As a reader, Graff made me uncomfortable, because I couldn't decide whether I liked or disliked him. Clearly he cared about Ender. He openly admitted it more than once, if not to Ender, then to others.

—

"He [Graff] can use anybody—below him or above him or complete strangers who've never met him—to accomplish whatever he thinks is needful for the human race."
—MAZER RACKHAM (in *Ender in Exile*)

—

---

[3] While in the hallway reading at 4:00 AM, I ate some leftover prime rib from dinner and got horseradish sauce in my sinuses right at the moment when Bean announced to Ender he had been named a team commander. My tears were from the horseradish. That's my story and I'm sticking to it.

Graff's motive was to save humanity. Does that justify taking a six-year-old genius, and putting him through a trial by fire to forge him into the greatest weapon mankind has ever known? Let's see…a single individual born to bear the burden of mankind's salvation…Well, to say the least, there's a cultural precedent! Still, it's an unsettling question—especially when the military is involved. We want to say that such an action is never justified, and yet our survival imperative says otherwise. It's easy for the people of Ender's world to call Graff evil or irresponsible in retrospect once the formics are gone, and humanity's greatest threat is once more itself.

Not only did the world condemn Graff, they condemned Ender as well—the very hero who saved them. In fact, Ender himself had a huge hand in painting his actions in a negative light, having penned *The Hive Queen*. It was a powerful choice Card made when he decided to have Ender go down in future history as a villain despised by good people everywhere. "Ender the Xenocide." Future history saw him as so evil, so iconic, that the action became the person. He became the embodiment of the very concept of species annihilation.

This was more than just an authorial choice, however; it was an epiphany. Of course the world would come to hate Ender! It had to! How else could humanity cope with the horrific cost of its own survival?

Who do we hate when a weapon of mass destruction leaves blood on our hands? When we dropped the atomic bombs on Hiroshima and Nagasaki, did we come to hate Einstein for coming up with the formula for nuclear fission? Did we hate Oppenheimer for building the bomb? Did we blot Truman's name from history for using it even though it wasn't necessary? No, because then we would be implicating ourselves as accomplices. So instead we hated the bomb.

When an act is perpetrated *by* us, rather than *upon* us, we tend to find a receptacle for our hatred that keeps our own consciences clean. We hate the weapon—and when that weapon is an individual, all the better.

—

"You had to be a weapon, Ender... functioning perfectly
but not knowing what you were aimed at."
—MAZER RACKHAM

—

In Ender's world, it was very clear that "Dr. Device" wasn't really seen as the weapon: Ender himself was. For the world to clear its conscience, and move beyond the formic extinction, there needed to be a scapegoat. Ender the Xenocide. With the blame cast firmly upon Ender, mankind was free to inherit the worlds and infrastructure left behind by the formics with impunity. To the victor goes the spoils of the stars.

If Ender's world didn't come to hate him, that would be a dark portent for humanity. It would mean that humanity approved of the xenocide. By distancing itself from what Ender did, humanity takes a step in the right direction. Were we as enlightened as the hive queen, we wouldn't need a scapegoat. We would come to terms with our own actions, and accept the blame. But alas, we are not. So we blame Ender.

On the other hand, Ender does become more enlightened than his society. Rather than hating Graff for his many deceptions, Ender understands him, and even becomes his friend. In *Speaker for the Dead* and in subsequent books of the initial series, Ender even makes peace with his own vilification. He's able to go on in spite of what he's done and what the world thinks of him, mainly because Card offers Ender some mercy and a little bit of grace at the conclusion of *Ender's Game*. A hive queen, whose spirit somehow resonates in his mind, forgives him totally and completely for annihilating her species—and he's left with a formic pupa, the seed for rebirth. She feels no animosity, only an abiding sorrow that Ender can share.

—

What the hive queen felt was sadness, a sense of resignation. She had not thought these words as she saw the humans coming to kill, but it was in words that Ender understood her: The humans did not forgive us, she thought. We will surely die.

—

Yet forgiveness and hope is the gift given to Andrew Wiggin at the end of the book—and for Ender, that is the only forgiveness that matters. It ennobles him, and frees him to find a new destiny as a speaker for the dead: a religious figure of stoic truth and resolve, enlightened, sometimes tortured, yet finding a small measure of peace with what he has done, and the way the many worlds of humanity—worlds taken from the extinct formics—despise his very name.

Of course, we as readers don't hate Ender because we know his heart every step of the way. For this reason, we love Ender. Not just for everything he is but also for everything he isn't.

—

I am not a killer, Ender said to himself over and over. I am not Peter. No matter what Graff says, I'm not. I was defending myself.

—

He isn't Peter. He has no ambition for himself beyond survival. He doesn't take pleasure in destroying his enemy. His devastating victories against Stilson and Bonzo did not bring him any joy, nor did destroying the formics.

Ender himself had a powerful realization as to what he felt at the moment of victory: that what made him truly able to defeat any foe is that, at the moment of victory, he truly knew and loved his enemy.

To love your enemy is to suffer the pain of their defeat along with them. There is almost a divine aspect to that. In a sense, Ender sacrificed his soul so that mankind might live. Of course, he didn't know at the time that his greatest battle was real, but it doesn't lessen the power of the sacrifice he made. One can argue that he was just a victim of a duplicitous military—but never did he feel or behave like a victim. That refusal to be a victim elevates him to something of a saint. A martyr who became victory for humanity. Victory and shame.

———

Let everybody drink some of my sweat today.

———

Ultimately, Ender's innocence is his most valuable asset, even more so than his keen intelligence. We can say he was jaded and twisted by his experience in Battle School, but that wouldn't be true—because down to the end he maintained purity of spirit in the face of everything that was hurled at him. Ender, after everything, was still a child... and yet not—and therein lies the genius of Ender as a character. He enters the story at age six and completes his mission by age twelve, but he never sounds like a six-year-old, or a twelve-year-old for that matter. He doesn't quite sound like an adult either. He seems both jaded and innocent at the same time. He and the child characters around him are so unique that they are ageless.

Orson Scott Card did something remarkable; he turned Ender into the child that we become in our dreams when we find ourselves back in the sixth grade reliving the most traumatic moments of our youth. We are at once the child in the dream, and the adult of our waking life. For that reason, we can't help but deeply identify with Ender. He becomes for us not a real child but a mythic being very much like that dream-self, ageless yet eternally young. Wise, yet unjaded. Just as we identify with the Halfling whose simple innocence and purity allowed him to save the world from the evil of the One Ring, so are we touched by Ender, the mythic innocent destined to bear the weight of the world on his shoulders.

We embrace Ender because we want to believe with all of our hearts that the necessary act of survival can be done in innocence despite civilization's need to vilify and condemn the perpetrator. It's comforting to us as readers and accidental philosophers that we can still see Ender as a hero.

I'd go as far as to say that even Peter is ultimately a comforting character. With Peter, Card asks, "Can there be a benevolent megalomaniac?" Does absolute power corrupt absolutely? We've always been told that, but deep down we want to believe that the old adage is a lie, that maybe we can learn from our mistakes, that maybe even the worst of us can grow. It's reassuring to think that a sociopathic genius like Peter could find a way to align his own selfish goals with the goals of humanity and become the great unifier of all mankind.

That's the kind of thing that Orson Scott Card does best: forcing us to reevaluate the way we think about everything. He doesn't give us the all-too-familiar fallen hero but rather a true hero vilified. He doesn't give us the typical vision of a ruler corrupted, but instead shows us corruption turned to serve the greater good. Even when he had Valentine play the role of the frighteningly demagogic Demosthenes, while Peter played the role of conciliatory Locke, he was forcing us to see things a little differently, to see the irony of how the left and the right can collude to manipulate the public, and serve each other.

As mankind gains knowledge at an exponential rate, we struggle to find the wisdom with which to deal with that knowledge. More and more, we find crucial wisdom in stories like *Ender's Game*. We find within fictional characters

or in fictionalizations of real characters something that resonates as real in our souls. After all, a well-crafted biography
is not merely about facts, but about the heart and soul of
an individual, the world in which that person lived, and
how that world reflects our own. The identical is true of fiction—especially thought-provoking science fiction because
the arena lends itself so well to allegory.

What I see as the great hope for humanity is that we are
compelled to find new perspectives, and to look at complex
situations like those served to us by Orson Scott Card. For
a short time, we become Ender, grappling with that which
must be done versus that which is right to do—in this case,
the moral ambiguity of survival. The more we challenge
ourselves with literature that dares to pose the hard questions, the better equipped we are to navigate real-world
complexities.

In recent years, we've developed a deep fascination with
the understanding of not just heroes but of villains as well. The
humanizing of a serial killer, such as in *Dexter*. The turning of
Anakin Skywalker into Darth Vader. Even our obsession with
the show-stopping musical vindication of the Wicked Witch
speaks volumes about us. We, as a species, are beginning to
realize that good and evil are not so simplistically clear as we
once thought they were. Our eyes were opened by the likes
of Shakespeare (the bard, not the planet) to the vast complexity of the human condition, and finally we are truly ripe for
embracing it. We want our stories to show more than just the
dark and the light; we are compelled to explore the grays.
The intricacies of human existence, human choices, and human survival. Nowhere is that clearer than in *Ender's Game*.

—

"Human beings are free except when humanity needs them."

—HYRUM GRAFF

—

I've often wondered how the story would have gone if Ender knew that his final game was the actual war. Would he have gone through with it? Card answers the question in *Ender in Exile*. Ender says point blank that, yes, even if he knew, he would have tried to complete his mission, and end the formics to save humanity. I think it would have destroyed him, though. I suspect he would have found a way to end his own existence in the process of saving humanity, finding the weight of his harsh victory unbearable. He would have been a true tragic character.

But, on the other hand, I think Ender and Orson Scott Card are smarter than that. If Ender knew the final battle was real, I think he would have changed the game again, this time by changing the objective. Because if he truly was incapable of losing, wouldn't the greatest victory be to save and preserve both species in a lasting peace?

I believe if Ender knew what he was truly doing, he would have used the fleet to find a way to communicate with the formics, and ultimately he would have been successful enough to learn that they were no longer a threat. So perhaps the greatest failure in Ender's game was Graff's and Mazer's because, by not trusting Ender fully and completely enough to give him the full picture, they didn't allow Ender to work his magic. It was Ender's ability to see the big picture that made him a genius commander. With the whole picture, how gloriously he might have solved the problem!

Ah well. We'll never know. Except, perhaps, in an alternate Ender universe... which, come to think of it, is not entirely out of the question. After all, there are parallel novels in the Ender world—what would be wrong with adding one that is somewhat perpendicular?

I'd definitely stay up until four in the morning to read that.

Neal Shusterman is the award winning author of more then twenty young adult novels, including Everlost, Bruiser, Full Tilt, Downsiders, *and* Unwind—*which was selected by NPR as one of the top one hundred young adult novels of all time. His books have received numerous awards and honors in the US and internationally, including the* Boston Globe/Horn Book *award for* The Schwa Was Here. *His novel* UnWholly *premiered at number two on the* New York Times *bestseller list in August of 2012 in its category, and a film version of* Unwind *is currently in the works. Neal lives in Southern California and can be found at www.storyman.com.*

Q. Why did you have Bonzo Madrid and Ender fight to the death?

A. It was only with a feeling of dread and despair that I realized I had created a circumstance where no outcome other than a fight to the death was possible. Bonzo could not relent in his need to destroy Ender Wiggin; Ender, given the way he saw the world, could not defend himself with anything less than ultimate thoroughness. His goal was not to kill, but to render his enemy incapable of a second attack. But with Ender's smaller size and Bonzo's reliance on groups of thugs, Ender's only hope of victory was to isolate Bonzo by Bonzo's own decision, and then prevail quickly and thoroughly by attacking the most vulnerable points on Bonzo's body. Pain can be recovered from; only serious injury could stop the next attack.

When I understood this, I also understood that this was a terrible act; and while Ender did not *know* that he had killed Bonzo, he also did not know, going in, that he was *not* going to kill him. Ender also knew that Bonzo might very well kill him—he had threatened to do so—and he knew that more was at stake than his own survival. Ender understood better than anyone but Graff that only Ender Wiggin had any hope of being ready to command the human fleet against the formics. If he allowed Bonzo to damage or kill him, Ender would be allowing the formics to fight a human fleet commanded by someone who was less than the best humanity had available. That was not vanity or arrogance, but the obvious extrapolation from what Ender had achieved and learned in Battle School.

Once I realized that I could not avoid this fight, and that it had to have the outcome it had, then all I could do was move forward. What I refused to do was make it an "accident" (Bonzo falls and hits his head on a sink) or pull the Hollywood trick of making the villain inadvertently destroy himself. This was a mini-war within a larger war, and war has its own terrible logic. If I was going to show war in all its brutality, I had to show that the commander—even if his naked body is his entire army and all its weaponry—must do what it takes to destroy the enemy's will and capacity to inflict further damage. Any lesser goal in war is a decision to lose, with all the consequences that loss entails.

So I made the stakes as clear as possible to the reader, and I showed that Ender Wiggin, a highly moral person, understood and bore the moral burden of the choice he made. That is how good people fight wars—they knowingly inflict terrible damage, and they bear the moral consequences of it. By analogy, Ender's acceptance of the cocooned hive queen is his Marshall Plan; as Churchill said of Eisenhower, "Never have I seen a man so staunch in pursuing the purpose in hand, so ready to accept responsibility for misfortune, or so generous in victory."

Not everything Ender did was noble, but everything he did was or seemed necessary, and he accepted the consequences of his actions even when they were unavoidable or inadvertent. In our imperfect world, that is usually as close to nobility as we can ever come.

—OSC

IF THE FORMICS LOVE THEIR CHILDREN TOO

Or, How I Was Ender's Gamed Into Reflecting on the Exigencies of War

KEN SCHOLES

O f all the other contributors to this collection of essays, I suspect that I have the distinction of being the last to the party when it comes to Orson Scott Card's classic science fiction novel, *Ender's Game*. The invitation came across my email in January 2012. There was only one real problem:

I had not read *Ender's Game*.

I had read Card's *Homecoming Saga* and enjoyed it thoroughly in the mid-nineties. And I'd relied upon his writing book, *How to Write Science Fiction and Fantasy*, when I came back to writing in my late twenties. I knew he was a helluva storyteller and I had many of his books in my growing collection that I just hadn't gotten to ... yet.

Fast-forward to January 2012 and the invitation to write the words you're now reading. Of course, I accepted. And immediately confessed, as I have to all of you now, that I had not yet read the book. But with that confession, I attached a modest proposal—what if I read the book as a first-timer coming to it now in this space and time and then construct my essay from that framework as a newcomer?

You're reading this now, so it must have worked.

Shortly after committing to the project, Nature conspired to assist as it will, and I took a tumble on one of our few snow days in northwestern Oregon. Stuck in bed with a bungled knee, I picked up my copy of *Ender's Game* and settled into a two-day ride that I've been pondering now for five months.

That it stayed with me for so long is the mark of a timeless book and this one has quite a track record—millions of copies sold, translated around the world, and reaching beyond the borders of genre to draw young readers not just to reading but to reading science fiction. I think this is because it resonates with the times we live in as much now as it did when it first appeared on the scene, and will likely keep doing so for years and years to come.

But more than that, *Ender's Game* resonated with me on some very deep, very personal levels.

—

"We share the same biology regardless of ideology. What might save us, me and you, is if the Russians love their children too."

—STING, "Russians"

When the novel *Ender's Game* was published, I had just turned seventeen years old. I was midway through my junior year of high school and convinced I was going to Eastern Washington University to major in Creative Writing when I graduated. I was reading and writing a lot of science fiction and fantasy and submitting those short stories for publication. The very first was called "The Attic," about an old man who was sitting on his porch in a quiet suburban neighborhood, going through a box of photographs and drinking lemonade on a summer day while he waited for the Soviet missiles to cross the polar ice caps and wipe out the United States. I had probably written a dozen stories at this point, sending some of them along to various magazines for publication. But I was just four months away from tossing the writing aside to pursue the ministry instead and five months from joining the US Naval Reserve to ship out for basic training the summer before my senior year. I was teaching myself to play Simon and Garfunkel songs on my guitar, but the big hit on the radio was Tears for Fears' "Everybody Wants to Rule the World."

And we knew they did. Especially across the world in the Evil Empire. The signs were all around us—movies, television, books, music. The Russians *were* coming.

Sting's album *The Dream of the Blue Turtles*, which included the poignant single "Russians," came out the summer that I was in Basic Training, burnt crisp by the San Diego sun, learning how to march, run, swim, float, put out fires. I was preparing to be a force for good against the Soviet Union after a lifetime of anxiety about the missiles we had pointed at one another…and a lifetime of books, movies, and songs that played upon those anxieties. Art had been busily exploring the end of the world in a brand-new way—one that did not involve gods but men, thanks to the advent of the atomic bomb.

There was a lot of fear in the world at that time, and *Ender's Game* dropped brilliantly into that pond. It completes what I think of as the Holy Trinity of military SF books written during the Cold War, standing alongside Heinlein's *Starship Troopers* and Haldeman's *The Forever War*. Only Card cut into the onion even a bit deeper ... and brought children into it.

Back then, at seventeen—definitely a child from the standpoint of where I sit now—I missed this book. And probably wouldn't have understood it at the time. Even a year later, when I transferred into the US Army and shipped out for West Germany, I wouldn't have come even close to grasping the power of this book. Despite the fact that I knew, as an eighteen-year-old parts clerk and soldier, that I had a twenty-four-hour life expectancy if the balloon went up and the Soviets invaded West Germany.

What if, *Ender's Game* asks, humanity was presented with a foe that didn't share its biology? What if that enemy was so alien to us that ideological differences paled compared to the threat they posed? And what if the only way our best military minds could conceive of beating this enemy was to raise up a child they could sharpen as their innocent weapon?

And what if the extinction of the human race was at stake?

Timely, resonant questions,' given how long we'd been in a Cold War that made the same threat of extinction.

Ender's Game won both the Hugo and the Nebula for that year— the two highest honors in the genre—and then Card went on to do it again the next year with his follow-up, *Speaker for the Dead.*

Like I said—resonant questions.

The Cold War is over now. A year after I returned from my tour of duty, the wall came down. And on September 11, 2001, we became afraid of a new enemy—one who flew passenger planes filled with men, women, and children into buildings filled with men, women, and children.

I remember watching it on the news that morning, mouth open wide and tears streaming down my face. I remember a sky completely empty of airplanes for days. I re member being afraid.

Not a Cold War but a different kind of war this time, one that played even more directly to fear . . . to terror. I think it shook us—and the world—to the core. My own books—and several of my short stories—are heavily influenced by 9/11. And my life as well, but I'll get to that in a bit.

Ender's Game translates perfectly into this context as well, and as a first-time reader here in 2012, eleven years after the Al Qaeda attacks on the World Trade Center and the Pentagon, I found a different experience than I ever could have had back in 1985.

Because there's more to the story. More to my context for *Ender's Game* when I finally came around to reading it. Four years earlier—nearly to the week as I sit down here to write this—in the spring of 2008 my family lost one of its best and brightest to this new war. My nineteen-year-old nephew—an Airborne combat medic just barely into his first tour of duty in Afghanistan. He was killed when an IED went off on the side of the road as his convoy passed by.

His name was Andrew.

—

> *"Peter, you're twelve years old. I'm ten. They have a word for people our age. They call us children and they treat us like mice."*
>
> —VALENTINE, *Ender's Game*

It is no wonder to me why *Ender's Game* does so well with YA audiences; the children Card writes are capable, strong, and real. They are obviously not all good. We see them at their best and worst—as bullies and heroes, friends and foes.

And the things that the adults in the novel force those children to endure—especially Ender—are horrific. But the adults are not doing it out of hatred; they despise what they do even as they believe there is a higher good to be served by it. A few children sacrificed to save the human race. Another "Cold Equation," like writer Tom Godwin's, only Ender is the stowaway in the airlock and the vaccine must be delivered.

Card lays this out before us and I never sensed he set out to answer the questions he raised. Instead, he let them ride forward with the reader, for the reader to process—and answer—at their own risk, and as I read it, within my own personal context, the book became alive to me and did what good books do—it made me think, it made me feel.

And a part of that context that we haven't talked about is a newer one for me, one rooted deep in emotion—my role as a father. In just a few months, my twin daughters turn three. They were a life-changer of unspeakable proportions, the best and scariest and hardest and most beautiful story I will ever be a part of. And you see, I'm wired to feel that way. It's the sequel to Nature's First Great Trick of Keeping Humans Around (yes, I'm talking about sex), the gosh-wow follow-up: little people who arrive and change your life in ways that are hard to explain fully unless you've been down that road. Pretty neat trick.

Something wacky happened when my kids were born; there was a shift in my reality. When I talk about it with other parents, they usually smile and nod their heads. When I heard Elizabeth's first cry, I felt a weird biological "click" inside my brain. And this new reality, a new and higher priority, was already firmly cemented into place before Rachel made a peep: I was a father and my children mattered more than anything, period. Keeping them alive and cared for in the world, preparing them for a successful, meaningful life, was my new mission, and I knew I would spend myself utterly to do so.

And it just simply ambushed me in a moment. Nature is sneaky that way.

One of the bizarre changes in me as a result of fatherhood is that it's even harder now to read books or watch programs where children are put at risk or killed. I have a visceral reaction now that I didn't used to have. So watching the way that the children were used in *Ender's Game* was tough on me.

Of course, seeing it on the news each day is even tougher.

Because, despite this biological click that so many parents report having, we have a pretty poor track record, overall, as a species when it comes to our offspring. It's only rather recently in our history that we've implemented laws to protect children from exploitation and abuse. And despite improvements all around the world, children continue to be used, abused, and killed. Especially during times of war.

Card's imagined future simply dresses it all up with higher stakes by bringing the children to the center of the stage. Ender is humanity's best hope for defeating its fearful enemy. And the questions Card raises for us about fear and war and how we use our children are all brought to a head by his sucker-punch ending.

The enemy is soundly defeated and the child who made that possible is soon confronted with the realization that the xenocide he's committed was unnecessary. The formics, once they had learned humans were a thinking species, had broken off their attacks and put their effort into understanding humanity—and, eventually, into making contact with Ender.

But fear had done what fear does best: it had blinded Graff and his people to everything but itself and that cost those on both sides of the table far more than was ever returned on the investment.

—

"I said I did what I believed was necessary for the preservation of the human race, and it worked; we got the judges to agree that the prosecution had to prove beyond the shadow of a doubt that Ender would have won the war without the training we gave him. After that, it was simple. The exigencies of war."

—GRAFF, *Ender's Game*

I am angry about the exigencies of war. I can't help it. This is what *Ender's Game* whispered to me when I came around to it at this season in my life: war costs too damned much.

And like the best of storytellers, Card shows us the cost to Ender and the others rather than trying to answer the questions raised by that cost. Humanity expands out into the territory of its fallen foe, unchanged by yet another war of the thousands in its history. Cast aside, Ender experiences a type of death as the full weight of what he's done—what he's been caused to do—settles upon him. And then, when the formics' final message reaches him and their future lies in his hands, Ender rises to new life as the Speaker for the Dead.

My Andrew didn't survive to learn something profound. I'm left pondering the exigencies of our war and finding nothing profound either, only tragedy. I have no idea what exact exigencies exist within the group of people who built and positioned the IED that killed my nephew, but I'm certain they believed that they, too, were doing what they had to. War is tricky that way; exigencies abound for all involved.

I'd like for us to outgrow it as a species.

We humans are inventive, amazing critters and I'm convinced that if we can teach ourselves to fly like birds, to swim like fish, to go to the moon even—then we can figure this one out at some point. I just have to believe that we are capable. That learning to work in collaborative community is where our future lies.

Not in war.

Not in fear.

—

*"We may be young but we're not powerless. We play by
their rules long enough, and it becomes our game."*
—VALENTINE, *Ender's Game*

After I finished *Ender's Game*, I sat with the feelings it evoked
for several weeks. My thoughts on what to say about the
book were scattered—a vague flickering of ideas about fear
and love and manipulation and the cost of war.

It brought me questions and I pondered them, wondering what it's all about. It took me straight into the recent
memories of my nephew's death, of the limousines we rode
in along a street lined with people waving flags, holding
signs that thanked us for his sacrifice. Of the rifles they fired
at his graveside. And it delivered me back to that Almighty
Click I experienced when I first met my children, that sure
and absolute sense that they were now what mattered most.

And when I look at my daughters, I can see that there's
a sub-text to the story here that holds the key to these questions about the exigencies of war. Despite the way these
children are used, and despite the fear that surrounds and
shapes them, they ultimately learn what they can from the
generation in power, see that which is lacking, and set out
to change it.

Peter unites the world after dividing it with Valentine
via their mock arguments. He uses the same justifications
as Graff—the salvation of humanity. And like Graff, he re-
sorts to manipulations and machinations, influencing the
world through written arguments between imaginary foes

in an effort to save it. He plays the adult's game until he owns it, but unlike his brother, Peter Wiggin isn't motivated by love.

Ender is different from Peter and that difference is apparent from the earliest pages of the book. Despite what he's forced to do, Andrew Wiggin maintains a sense of compassion and empathy as he learns the games put before him. And at the end of it all, Ender uses that same empathy to alchemize what he's learned into a book about the formics that changes humanity.

I do not think it's a coincidence, either, that storytelling becomes the vehicle through which that change seeps in. Storytelling has always given us the perfect sandbox to play with our ideas and explore our hopes…and our fears. We need our storytellers to bring us to the edge of these places, to lean us out into the questions in the hopes that, if enough of us ask, we'll find an answer and a better way. Because the stories they tell stay with us longer than any news story we read or watch. Our stories travel with us down decades that become millennia and change us.

Speaking of stories, I have a couple of two-year-olds who are going to need a bedtime story soon. I want it to be a tale of plenty and of walking in the shoes of others and never being too scared to ask questions and always knowing where home is.

When they are older and the game is theirs, they'll hear other stories that act as compass needles northward—stories like *Ender's Game*. They'll be shaped by the art they're exposed to. And as they find their voices, they will tell their own stories about what they've learned along the way, asking their own questions. Those stories will march out from their lives to touch other lives and spark other stories. Somewhere at the end of it, I think peace is waiting. It is the slow and upward spiral of our species.

Ken Scholes *is the critically acclaimed author of three novels and over thirty short stories. His series* The Psalms of Isaak *is being published both at home and abroad to award nominations and rave reviews.* Publishers Weekly *hails the series as a "towering storytelling tour de force" in starred reviews of the first three volumes. Ken lives in Saint Helens, Oregon, with his wife, Jen West Scholes, and his twin daughters, Lizzy and Rae. He invites readers to look him up at www.kenscholes.com and follow his antics on Facebook.*

Q. What is Alai's surname? You haven't mentioned it in the book.

A. Not every culture has or requires surnames.

—OSC

Q. Why did you not have Ender lose at least one battle in the Battle Room?

A. Because the teachers were not trying to make him fail. They were trying to help him learn how to respond to unusual circumstances. Ender had been given a superb, hand-picked army, consisting of soldiers whose virtues all the other commanders (except Bean, not yet a commander) had overlooked. They stacked the deck *in his favor*, provided Ender had the wit to see what he had and use it.

Likewise, the battles in which they seemed to be cheating against him—facing two armies, the late notification, having too many battles in a row—were really circumstances that benefitted him, if he saw how to exploit the situation.

Facing two armies that could not work as a coherent unit left Ender outnumbered, but with some clear advantages, as his opponents vied with each other to fall into his trap. Facing an army that was able to establish itself first in the field of battle worked to his advantage because his opponent was incompetent and arrayed himself with as much stupidity as the French at Agincourt.

His exhausted army quickly became the most cohesive, experienced veterans in Battle School; they never lost their focus. It worked to Ender's advantage, even if he did not see it.

The teachers did not want Ender to fail; they wanted him to learn. He learned; he won. If he had ever lost a battle it would have shown that he was *not* ready to lead the International Fleet, because with all his advantages Ender *should* not have lost. That was what Graff was doing, and it worked.

—OSC

ENDER'S GAME: A GUIDE TO LIFE

MATT NIX

A dmit it: you were Ender.

You know what I'm talking about. When you read *Ender's Game* for the first time, you didn't say to yourself: "What an interesting exploration of the interior life of a young warrior-in-training!" You read it the way every true devotee of the novel does—with the secret knowledge that you were reading about yourself.

I read *Ender's Game* as a teenager after a close friend handed it to me and demanded that I start it immediately. I devoured it in a single sitting and then re-read it many times. It was a little different each time, but I always had the sense that it wasn't just a novel: it was a *guide to life*. No, that's not specific enough—it was *a guide to* my *life*.

As a writer myself, I know this has something to do with the particular literary technique used in the novel. We spend the entire story in Ender's head. We see the world through his eyes. The lessons he learns are the lessons we learn. But a trick of narrative perspective doesn't explain everything. *Remembrance of Things Past* takes place largely in the main character's head, but I didn't spend my youth imagining myself eating cookies in early-twentieth-century France. For some reason, I looked at this unhappy six-year-old who saves the world only to live the rest of his life in lonely isolation and said…, "I want some of *that*."

I recently turned forty. I have a career and a family. I just read *Ender's Game* to my oldest son, and will be reading it to my other two children soon enough. With the novel fresh in my mind, I think it's an appropriate time to re-examine some of the lessons I drew from it twenty-five years ago. Is it a good guide to life, or not? We shall see.

Lesson One: You are the single most important young genius on Earth. This fact will soon be recognized, and your destiny will be revealed.

Okay, just to be clear: I'm not saying I actually *believed* I was the smartest kid on Earth. I knew kids who were smarter than I was. And even by the standards of *Ender's Game* itself, I had already missed the mark by the time I read the book— I did nothing truly world-shaking before puberty. The closest I came to Ender-like brilliance was programming a version of "Space Invaders" on a TRS-80 personal computer when I was eleven. But did I believe I was destined for greatness? Hell, yes! I was intensely ambitious, but I was possessed of a lot more drive than direction. I didn't know what I was supposed to be doing, precisely, but I knew that it was something Very, Very Important. And so I waited. I waited for my Colonel Graff to come and tell me what it was I was supposed to be doing, what this fire burning in my guts was *for*. I knew it wouldn't be easy. I knew that I might not even want to follow the call of duty when it came. But at least the questions would be resolved, and I would know what I was destined for. It was a terrible realization for me (reached sometime in my twenty-fourth year) that with respect to Colonel Graff, *Ender's Game* had steered me wrong. No one was ever going to come along and *force* me to live up to my potential. It scared the hell out of me—not because I was afraid of working hard, but because I was deathly afraid of looking stupid. And isn't that what we're all afraid of, deep down? Consider how different *Ender's Game* would be if there had been no monitor, no tests, and no Hyrum Graff. Imagine if Ender had had to *volunteer* to go to Battle School. Imagine his letter to the Strategos: "Hi, my name is Ender Wiggin. You don't know me, but I'm pretty sure I'm the one you're looking for to save mankind." It would have been less exciting but a lot more like real life. In real life, you have to go out and find what you *think* is your destiny, and risk looking like an idiot if you're wrong. Ender had it hard, but he didn't have to lie awake at night, wondering, "Am I fooling myself? Maybe I should just go to law school instead." So did this first "lesson" steer me wrong? I'd have to say yes and no. Certainly it led me to believe fervently in destiny, even if my Graff-driven version would prove to be a fantasy. Eventually, I got impatient waiting for Graff to open the door and push me through it, and I did what we all must do: I opened the damn door myself. As for being the most important young genius on Earth, well . . . I suppose I have to acknowledge that, although I love my career, making TV may not be that important. Then again, you never know. It's possible my broadcast signals are being picked up by aliens, who are re-evaluating their invasion plans because Earth is seemingly populated with lots of bad-ass guys with guns and cool sunglasses.

Some fantasies die hard.

Lesson Two: Your pain has a purpose. Your suffering and loneliness are the keys to your greatness.

There's something about Ender's particular brand of isolated, vaguely superior loneliness that is almost impossible not to identify with. It's not an accident that the book is so popular with gifted kids who have discovered that being good at school doesn't necessarily make them popular. Ender spends a lot of his time feeling small, powerless, ashamed, bullied, even evil—but his trials invariably make him better. This was an important one for me. I was not a particularly unhappy teenager, at least as teenagers go. But I was a nerd, with the alienation and angst of the nerd. There was the occasional bully. I worked really hard in school, and it was exhausting sometimes. When I entered the working world, my first jobs were intense and difficult and depressing.

Through it all, though, I had Ender. I knew that, although I might not understand precisely what my current suffering was *for*, it was going to be useful someday. It would make me stronger. Eventually, I would be called upon to save the world—or something very close to it—and I would be ready. My reaction to that kid who used to push me around in P.E. class was Very, Very Important. It was a test, a critical waypoint on my path to...wherever I was going. My cool self-control might, to the untrained eye, have looked a lot like sullen, fearful resentment, but I knew better. It was a mark of greatness.

It may sound like pretentious self-delusion, and in some ways it was. But I think people underestimate the importance of pretentious self-delusion—or, at least, of using fantasy to help yourself through hard times. As we experience it, most suffering is pretty banal. Some kid pushes you around in P.E., and you stare at the floor in silent fury. You *could* be a humiliated fifteen-year-old who didn't stand up for himself in the locker room after gym class...or you could be Ender, learning important lessons by dealing with Peter, the young psychopath.

This wasn't just helpful when I was young and preparing for life. Humiliations and challenges, surprisingly enough, didn't end when I left school. In my first full-time job, I was making terrible money working for a talent agent who liked to call me names and hurl things in my direction when he got frustrated. It sucked. I considered leaving the entertainment industry entirely, but...there was always Ender. Was answering phones and making copies at a mid-level Hollywood talent agency really worse than Battle School? Perhaps the Screaming Agent was my own personal Bonzo Madrid. I would learn from his mistakes. I would be forged in the crucible of that agency and emerge stronger. Maybe I would even get to kill him someday.

It was a comforting thought, and it kept me at my desk, working hard through a misery that, on its face, wasn't particularly ennobling. But staying at that sorry desk was one of the most important decisions I ever made. It led me to a life, a family, and a career that I love.

At the same time, I've realized that my early understanding of this particular lesson was … not wrong exactly but incomplete. Suffering, by itself, is just suffering. A guy throwing a script at you because the fax machine is broken isn't *really* a lesson, any more than Ender's torment at Bonzo's hands was. Lessons are only lessons if you choose to see them that way. In some ways, wasn't that really Ender's greatest skill—his ability to learn from his torment? I mean, his greatest skill besides being a super-genius at age six with incredibly quick reflexes, a natural athleticism, and an effortless understanding of military strategy? You get the point.

Lesson Three: At the end of the day, the only thing anyone cares about is whether you won.

There's something wonderfully straightforward about an interstellar war against a horde of merciless, unknowable aliens. Certainly, it has its disadvantages—the senseless deaths, the blood and treasure poured into the void of space—but it does brings a certain *focus* to everything, doesn't it? Ender has to defeat the formics. Everything must be in service to that single goal, and in the end nothing much matters except which side is dead.

I never had a Formic War to fight in (tragically), but I was pretty enchanted with this philosophy nonetheless. As far as I was concerned, *Ender's Game* made it pretty clear that the ends justified the means. Ender did real damage to people, but he *had* to. He bent rules and did away with civilized norms of behavior in the Battle Room, but that was the key to his victory. At the end of the book, when the only way to win was by violating the ultimate taboo against destroying an entire species, well...he did what he had to do. He's hailed as a hero, and nobody worries too much about broken taboos.

It's a seductive philosophy when you're fifteen years old. It's a great justification for cheating on a French test, anyway. I had Very Important Things to do with my life, and if I had to break a few rules to get the grades that would get me into the best college and launch me on my way, so be it! Millions of lives might be at stake!

Fortunately, I didn't have the stomach to adopt this mindset wholeheartedly. I felt guilty when I wrote the answers to my French vocabulary quizzes on the desk, even though Madame Stillman didn't notice. Also, there was the issue of not really knowing what rules to break in order to facilitate my rise to greatness and crush my enemies. Ender had these awesome flashes of brilliance, but it came a little harder for me. I'd stand on the basketball court at lunchtime, racking my brain for some stroke of tactical genius that would allow me to destroy the other team. I never came up with much, and while I was thinking, the other team was usually scoring.

Still, I kept this lesson close to my heart. In his last battle, Ender thinks, "I don't care if I follow your rules. If you can cheat, so can I. I won't let you beat me unfairly—I'll beat you unfairly first." I knew that at some point I, too, was going to have to get ruthless. I would have to break some arms. I would leave bodies in my wake. It might not be pretty, but at the end of the day, after some unspecified victory, all would be forgiven, as it had been for Ender. I conveniently ignored the obvious flaw in my thinking, which was that Ender thought he was playing a game in that battle, while I was imagining this as a roadmap for life.

Here's the other problem: Ender's victory over the formics isn't the end of the book, even if it felt that way at fifteen. At a time in my life when the approval of others seemed like pretty much the only thing that mattered, being hailed as a hero by all mankind seemed like a good gig, no matter what it took to get there. But as the book takes pains to make clear, that's not necessarily the case. Ender, the tool of Graff and Mazer Rackham, is wracked with guilt. Ender, the miracle-worker, can never go home again. Ender, the legend, can never have a real life. He has to live in the future, as the Speaker for the Dead, dealing with the moral implications of his actions. So…oops.

Still, there is a yet deeper truth here, one that *has* been an important part of my life and career. At the end of the day, you have to deliver the goods, and people don't much care how you feel about it. Ender suffers for all of his victories. He feels guilt for the people he hurt. He feels terrible about sacrificing his teammates. He regrets exterminating the formics. He had a job to do, he had choices to make, and he had to *live with his choices for the rest of his life.* We all do.

In my current career in television, there's a cold calculation at work. If your audience numbers are high enough, you stay on the air, and if they aren't, you're out. It doesn't matter how you feel about it, whether you played by the rules, or how nice you were to people along the way. They count the eyeballs and they make a decision.

In the war for eyeballs, I've won and I've lost. In victory, everybody makes money, and you are hailed as a hero. In defeat, well...there's nothing quite like seeing something with your name on it being rejected by millions of people. The stakes may be slightly lower than they are in an interstellar war against hostile aliens, but they're high enough. Under such circumstances, you have to make hard choices, choices that will sometimes cause pain. Unfortunately, *not* making the choices will cause pain too. So there. You want to be in charge? Deal with it.

And so, at this point in my life, I find myself drawing a modified, and somewhat more painful, version of this lesson from the book. The ends *don't* justify the means. Nothing justifies anything. There's just what you do, and whether you can live with it. It may be true that the only thing anyone *else* cares about is whether you won, but that doesn't mean it's the only thing that matters.

And so, Madame Stillman, wherever you are, I'm sorry I cheated on that French test. It was my fault, not Ender's.

Lesson Four: Your people are out there. You may feel alone now, but be patient, and you will find them.

For most of the novel, Ender Wiggin is a pretty isolated fellow. He's got Valentine, and some intermittent friendships, but with Colonel Graff rearranging things at Battle School, he isn't able to make many close pals. He's lonely, and that loneliness only deepens over the course of the book.

And yet...I remember how it felt, reading about Battle School for the first time. I remember how profoundly I longed to be there. Yes, Ender was lonely, but he'd found his people—he was in a place where he was appreciated, and known. He had his squad, he had his army, and in the later books, his jeesh. The closest I could get to that was the other dorks in the theater club. They were my friends, sure, but would they die for me?

Ender gave me faith that things would change. I would find my people too. Tragically, I had been born too early to find them in Battle School, but...maybe somewhere? In college? Or at work?

The reality was disappointing. I had a little luck finding my people in an academic summer camp I attended, but it was all too brief. College was UCLA—a great school, but it's hard for twenty-two thousand undergraduates to cohere into a band of brothers. As for the workplace, well...apparently corporations are primarily interested in *making money*, not in fostering a deep camaraderie among the employees.

But this one was a hard dream to give up. So hard, in fact, that I didn't give it up, even in the face of quite a bit of evidence that it was just a juvenile fantasy. And for a long time, it stayed that way.

Over time, though, a funny thing happened. "My people" started showing up. The more I dedicated myself to the things I really cared about, the more I ran into kindred spirits. These were the people who really *would* fight alongside me. It has been one of the great joys of my life that I have found a career where I can surround myself with extremely talented people who are all devoted to a common goal. I found my army—and it turned out to be filled with a lot of—guess what?—theater dorks. So far, no one has died for me, but then again, I haven't asked.

Interestingly, my life has also turned out to be filled with other *Ender's Game* fans. Over the years, I have learned to recognize my brothers and sisters. You know what I'm talking about: you meet someone, and without even asking the question, you just *know* you've found a fellow fan. I have more than one brother-in-arms who I found *because of the book that sold me on the idea of having brothers-in-arms.* Which is kind of awesome, in my opinion.

Through these people, I've also learned I wasn't alone in looking to *Ender's Game* as a guide. I've seen how their own understanding of the book has evolved. That's as it should be, I think—there are lessons to be learned in *Ender's Game*, but they are learned less *from* the book than *with* it. You keep your dog-eared copy as you move through life, thumbing through it at key moments, finding new things. The text becomes part of you, while the book itself binds you to all the others making their way through life with *their* dog-eared copies of *Ender's Game*.

For me, the deepest validation of this lesson came some years ago, when I chanced upon a review of my show *Burn Notice* that had been written by none other than Orson Scott Card. I immediately told a member of my writing staff, with whom I had connected largely because he had read *Ender's Game* more than a hundred times. He immediately told his writing partner, whom he had met in college, when they bonded over a mutual love of... *Ender's Game*.

I wrote to Orson, and he wrote back. We stayed in touch, and I met him earlier this year. It was a profound experience for me, and confirmed the role of the novel in my life the way that nothing else could have. Orson Scott Card wrote a book that helped to inspire my life and career and guided me to a place that led me all the way back to Orson Scott Card.

And if that's not finding your people, I don't know what is.

Matt Nix is the creator and executive producer of the one-hour action drama Burn Notice, *currently in its sixth season on the USA Network. He also created the action-comedy* The Good Guys *for the Fox Network. He is the author of several feature film scripts currently languishing in various states of development at major studios. He lives in Los Angeles with his wife, three children, and dog.*

ABOUT THE EDITOR

Orson Scott Card is the author of the novels *Ender's Game*, *Ender's Shadow*, and *Speaker for the Dead*, which are widely read by adults and younger readers, and are increasingly used in schools.

His most recent series, the young adult Pathfinder series (*Pathfinder*, *Ruins*) and the fantasy Mithermages series (*Lost Gate*, *Gate Thief*) are taking readers in new directions. Besides these and other science fiction novels, Card writes contemporary fantasy (*Magic Street*, *Enchantment*, *Lost Boys*), biblical novels (*Stone Tables*, *Rachel and Leah*), the American frontier fantasy series The Tales of Alvin Maker (beginning with *Seventh Son*), poetry (*An Open Book*), and many plays and scripts, including his "freshened" Shakespeare scripts for *Romeo and Juliet*, *The Taming of the Shrew*, and *The Merchant of Venice*.

Card was born in Washington and grew up in California, Arizona, and Utah. He served a mission for the LDS Church in Brazil in the early 1970s. Besides his writing, he teaches occasional classes and workshops and directs plays. He frequently teaches writing and literature courses at Southern Virginia University.

Card currently lives in Greensboro, North Carolina, with his wife, Kristine Allen Card, where his primary activity is feeding birds, squirrels, chipmunks, possums, and raccoons.

ACKNOWLEDGMENTS

The publisher extends their sincerest thank you to all the Ender fans who submitted their thoughtful questions for the Q&As in this book, especially:

3dcivilwar	for-bittenlove	Carlos Ramirez
acanofdietorangeslice	Brian Johnson	Reginald Linsao
achillesdeponies	melissakohler	Elizabeth C. Spencer
Angel Co	Jason R. Morales	Jonathan Tillman
internet-haze	mpolluxork	

and

Czhorat	hikaruchord	Gudrún Saga
diamond-standard	James Kamlet	Danion Sisler
easternwu	McDermott	Ssmith
Enderspeaker	Bryan Morrison	Tblondin
freefoodatpenn	Nathan Neufeld	theawkwardchild
Declan M. Garrett	Orion	Emily Thorpe
Paul Graham	Iván Preuss	unlockthesecret
Megan Grazman	Ruthie	

Many thanks, also, to the Ender fansites that helped us get the word out, all great sources of Ender book and movie news:

EndersAnsible.com
EnderNews.com
EnderWiggin.net

WANT MORE HUNGER GAMES?

THE GIRL WHO WAS ON FIRE
MOVIE EDITION

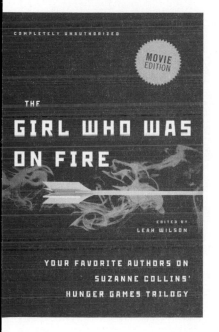

"*The Girl Who Was on Fire* is a MUST read for any Hunger Games fan…As touching and thought provoking as the series itself…[the] essays included will challenge you to think of the trilogy in a new and deeper way…the Hunger Games may be over, but thanks to *The Girl Who was on Fire*, the discussion continues." —**Down With the Capital fansite**

"Discussing the philosophy that lies beneath [*The Hunger Games*] film, the characters within, and allegories of society, Leah Wilson and sixteen writers of young adult fiction come together and provide much to think about with the work. *The Girl Who Was on Fire* is well worth considering for fans." —**Midwest Book Review**

"I thoroughly enjoyed every single essay…My copy is completely highlighted, underlined, written in the margins, and dog-eared. You don't know how many times while I was reading it I said emphatically to myself, 'Yes!!' as I underlined or highlighted a quote or passage." — **Book Nerds Across America**

Read a FREE EXCERPT from *The Girl Who Was on Fire* at:
HTTP://WWW.SMARTPOPBOOKS.COM/HUNGERGAMES

SARAH REES BRENNAN	NED VIZZINI	BRENT HARTINGER
JENNIFER LYNN BARNES	CARRIE RYAN	SARAH DARER LITTMAN
MARY BORSELLINO	CARA LOCKWOOD	JACKSON PEARCE
ELIZABETH M. REES	DIANA PETERFREUND	ADRIENNE KRESS
LILI WILKINSON	TERRI CLARK	BREE DESPAIN
	BLYTHE WOOLSTON	

WANT MORE SMART POP?

WWW.SMARTPOPBOOKS.COM

» Read a new free essay online everyday
» Plus sign up for email updates, check out our upcoming titles, and more

Find Smart Pop Online:

 Become a fan on Facebook:
FACEBOOK.COM/SMARTPOPBOOKS

 Follow us on Twitter:
@SMARTPOPBOOKS